Ma.
7.9 2023

One Year is not enough

enough

50 years a Battersea youth worker

by Robert Musgrave

Independently published by Providence and Shallowford
Publishing

This book is dedicated to Susan,

partner in faith and work and love for over forty years,

and critical friend in the writing of this book.

Table of Contents

Preface

This book is a tapestry about Providence House, Clapham Junction, Battersea. About me and my part in its story, about East Shallowford Farm and the Shallowford Trust, because it all weaves in together, my life, Providence House, East Shallowford.

In 1978, Elizabeth Braund, having lived at East Shallowford for a couple of years, sat down to write her book about Providence House, its origins, her story and her part in it. The book is called 'The Young Woman who lived in a Shoe'. Although she did write short pieces and spoke about it on many occasions, she didn't write another book, either about Providence House or East Shallowford. That has been left to me.

This book, One Year is not enough, is not a sequel to the Young Woman, although in a way it is. More it is my book, my take, my close to hand perspective over fifty years. My older brother Peter said I should call it 'The Young Man who couldn't get out of the Shoe', and in a way, he is right because Providence House was a shoe I couldn't get out of, but you know the saying that if a shoe fits...

This book begins in 1973, and it ends in 2023, but it hasn't ended, because the story continues and some of it untold. This book doesn't follow a chronological sequence, so in one chapter you could find us ranging between the decades to follow a theme.

A brief timeline to bear in mind as you join the journey.

1963 Elizabeth Braund establishes The Providence House Trust in Speke Road, Battersea.

1969 Elizabeth Braund establishes The Providence House Youth Club Trust

1970 New Providence House building opens on Falcon Road, Battersea.

1973 Robert Musgrave arrives as a residential volunteer.

1975 Elizabeth Braund and Rosemary Bird begin The Lung for the City project on Dartmoor, Devon.

1976 Purchase of East Shallowford Farm, Widecombe in the Moor, Devon.

1976 Robert Musgrave appointed Senior Youth Worker, seconded by ILEA.

1983 Robert and Susan marry.

2002 Elizabeth Braund establishes The Shallowford Trust, and registers it as charity in 2004.

2010 Rosemary Bird dies.

2012 Robert Musgrave retires from the Youth Service

2012 Esther Clevely appointed Senior Youth Worker

2013 Elizabeth Braund dies.

2022 Robert Musgrave retires from operational activities at Providence House.

I am more than grateful to Susan Musgrave for examining each chapter as I wrote them and signposting me to some different approaches.

I am grateful to David Stone of Big Local SW11, Esther Clevely of Providence House and Dennis Eno a life-long Providence House member for scrutinising the draft copy, and adding comments for the back cover.

I am grateful to my brother Andrew for help with preparing the book for publication, Chike Chiejine, connected to Providence since his teenage years, for designing the cover, and most grateful to you, who have the book in your hand.

I hope you enjoy being part of the story.

Robert Musgrave MBE.

April 2023.

Chapter 1:

One year is not enough.

It was the early hours of the morning and there was noise and shouting and swearing outside the window, and then a crash. I gingerly looked up from my top bunk through the little window to see a man, I later came to know as Lewey, hurling one of those metal street bins through the window of the green grocers, just a few yards away across the pedestrian passageway, that ran between the row of shops on one side and Providence House on the other.

What was I supposed to do?

Fortunately, I was saved by the equally alarming bellow of Elizabeth Braund from somewhere higher up in the building, and it all calmed down. Elizabeth Braund, the founder of Providence lived in a flat above the club. I was to hear Elizabeth's trenchant voices many more times in the months and years to come.

I got to know Lewey, a local character, whose children eventually all attended the youth club at some point or other. When he was drunk, he remembered his grievances very vividly and smashed the windows of the offending tradespeople. Thus he felt aggrieved by the undertakers, the betting office and the pub, but fortunately not Providence House. Lewey had a good tenor voice when drunk, and I remember his serenading me more than once while under the influence.

That was my first night, as far as I can remember. It was a Tuesday. My bedroom was little more than a cupboard. It was then called the hostel room, in case any young person, having been rendered temporarily homeless, needed a bed for the night. It is now our administration office. The only other furniture was a slim-framed bunk bed, an unvarnished bedside two drawer cabinet and a recess with a rail for any jackets to hang on. The room looked even smaller, as there was an angled wall the other side of which was the outside refuse cupboard. This meant that at least once a week there was an early morning call, as the dustcart pulled up in the forecourt, and the steel paladin bin was creakily withdrawn, emptied and returned with a clash and a clang.

That was my first night, but I lived for several years in the 'cupboard', at times with a fellow traveller, and for one night with a lad Elizabeth took pity on. I discovered that my purse was lighter when he left the next day. In addition to my 'cupboard' there was a two-bedroomed first floor flat at Providence, where Elizabeth Braund and Rosemary Bird, the second in command at Providence House, lived. I too graduated upstairs to live in the flat above, once Elizabeth had started the farm project on Dartmoor, and thus I lived on the job for ten years, until Susan and I were married.

I only came for one year in July 1973. I only came for one year, but somehow, I have never found the exit. Fifty years on I am still involved in Providence House, still actively participating in this Battersea community, and it has long become a part of my life, just as Providence House became a part of so many lives.

I had come to Providence House in search of a year's voluntary work, which we might call a gap year today. I was in my final year of an honours degree in History with Philosophy at the University of Kent in Canterbury, and had no idea where I should be going with my life. The circumstances that connected me to Providence House I regard as providential, and indeed providence has been a determining factor in my experience throughout my years at Providence.

I attended as a student a small independent chapel in Barton Road, Canterbury, and the pastor of the church there had been invited as a visiting speaker at a church in Chessington, which was holding a weekend of meetings in the late spring of 1973. Another of the invited guests was Elizabeth Braund of Providence House. In all the years I knew her, I could probably count on one hand the number of times she undertook such outside engagements to talk about the work at Providence House. She spoke movingly and challengingly about the work with young people in Battersea, after which my minister, John White, brightly went up to her and said that he knew of a young man who might be willing to come and help.

He got the telephone number right, but Elizabeth's surname wrong, and as I was to discover later so did many others – Braund, Prawn, and 'Prawnies Club' which was an affectionate way of describing Providence. I cranked up my motorbike (an Aerial Arrow 200), and found my way to Battersea, first getting lost in Clapham, and sat with Elizabeth and heard of the opportunities and challenges. I came away with the feeling that here was something I could be a part of. I came to Providence with a commitment to stay for one year in 1973 – it has been a long year!

This was the deal at Providence House. They would feed me and accommodate me, but if I needed money, then I should go out and find a morning job locally. I tramped the streets of old Battersea day after day in the first week of September, but to no avail. Morgan's Crucible, Garton's Glucose, Price's Candles, Delta, names mostly now living in the memory – none of them wanted morning work only. Woolworths at the Junction did, however, and I began to unload lorries, and sort incoming supplies into appropriate departments. I did this for two years. In fact, I was quite good at it and the manager at one point offered me a permanent job. I turned it down.

I am not really a proper Londoner, but have become one. My childhood was spent in Croydon, and my youth in East Sussex, with a view of the South Downs in the distance out of the back windows of the house in Heathfield; and every time I travel by train or car and nestle close to those old green hills of the Downs, I feel the pull and plaintive call to return; but I didn't. I do believe that my coming to London at 21 years of age was a providence, literally, in that that was when I first came to Providence House, and also because the circumstances of my choice were providential.

I believe in providence - obviously in that I believe in Providence House, otherwise I should not have been there for so long – 50 years and counting. I believe in providence, in that there is a sense of guidance in life, a sense of there being put in the way during the course of one's life, for good or for ill, or to make good of what seems ill. Indeed, the choice that sealed the course of my working life came as far as I am concerned by the hand of providence. It was in the summer of 1976.

I had been living in my 'cupboard' for almost three years now, and at the end of each year, felt I needed to stay for longer. At the end of my second year, I was encouraged to acquire some professional training, and look beyond the loading bay at Woolworths. I enrolled with a graduate teaching course that started in September 1975, and sought to balance the learning at college with full on Providence House duties. The balance was thrown out of kilter in October, when the project that Elizabeth Braund had been working towards, 'A Lung for the City', suddenly took off, and she and Rosemary set off to Dartmoor to establish the farm project, that would change all of our lives.

I was left to try and hold things together, with a very part-time team of volunteers. Somehow it sort of worked. I was doing the crazy thing of studying to be a teacher in the day at college, rushing back to Providence to get ready to open the club in the evening.

Every evening including the late-night Friday dances, as well as youth football Saturdays and Sunday school Sundays. Apart from Mondays, the place was heaving with young people every night.

At this time, I did not feel ready to leave Providence – an unsettling feeling that has an enduring quality. Meanwhile I had secured a position as a part time teacher in a school in Pollards Hill to start in the September, but had yet to confirm my acceptance. I am not sure how it would have worked out.

One Wednesday evening during the youth club in that hot summer of '76, Elizabeth Braund, up from her duties at the farm, asked me whether, if I were offered a position as a youth worker by the local authority, I would take it in order to be able to work at Providence full time. I said that of course I would think about it. That came out of the blue. Half an hour later there was a phone call from the headmaster of the school offering me the teaching place, and he wanted to know if I still wanted the job. I said "No," and made my choice. I chose my path. The timing was unnervingly providential. Or could say assuredly providential. Within months, I was a paid, full-time youth worker under the Inner London Education Authority, seconded to work at Providence House. When Wandsworth Borough Council took over the youth service in 1990, I moved over to their payroll, until they decided to cut the posts at most of the community-based youth centres in 2012. I am grateful to them, and more so, grateful to the providence of God. The providence to me was in the sense of timing. Had Elizabeth not had that conversation with me that night, I might well have said yes to the teaching job, because it would have been a way of keeping me at Providence House. That would have been a difficult thing to do, holding down a job and running Providence at the same time. This other way was a better way. I see it as a providence.

Essentially, I am quite a shy person, and somehow I made my way among the people at Providence House, and in the area. I suppose I never represented a threat, or ever looked remotely in those days like a professional; but I got to know people. I remembered their names. I stayed around. I wasn't here this year and then gone forever. I hung around. I sort of lasted and that has given me a platform. Even today almost every single week someone from the past who remembers their younger days returns, and behold I am still here – though less so routinely now.

I was asked by a man whose association with Providence House was even earlier than mine, whether I knew from the beginning if this would be my life's work, and I said "No." I never had a flash of light, a blinding vision, but just a growing something, inside, that this was where I was meant to be, that this is where I had something to do. It has always been people that have sustained my interest and kept me going. I have kind of grown up in this work

I began by working alongside people my own age, those only a few years younger than me, some a bit older; then seen them grow up, then seen their children, and even in some cases their children's children. I have been at Providence as a young man finding who I was, as a man, as a husband, as a father, and now as some old geezer who can no longer keep pace with the youngsters. I have worked with many people over many years, the good, the bad and the ugly, and with people who have made an impact on my life, and I trust I have made some impression on their lives. With all I have found there to be some connection. I attended a funeral recently, and one of the mourners spoke of how influential Providence and the farm had been in his life. I almost groaned, as I told him what a trial, he had been to us. The groan turned to a smile. We exchanged phone numbers.

I have often been asked what is the secret to going on, to keeping young, which is a weird perception, and I often throw out the glib comment that it is young people who keep me young, or that the Lord gives me strength, both of which have some truth. I think the thing that has sustained me is the scriptures, by the grace of God. It is the Bible. I may not have been the man of prayer I should have, nor the communicator I might have been, nor the one for church gatherings I might have been committed to; but I have found something in this book, in God's Word, and that in itself is another providence. Almost every day there is a word, a phrase, a sentence, a story that resonates with something in my life, or in the world around.

One of the most telling phrases for me was an expression in the book of Ezra: 'And now for a little space, grace has been shown from the Lord our God, … to give us a nail in his holy place, that our God may lighten our eyes, and give us a little reviving in our struggles.' [1] I felt that I had a place, like a nail or a peg that holds down the curtains or whatever. I had a place in the scheme of things. In Providence. In Battersea. In God's work.

I found that without question - one year was not enough.

Footnote

[1] Ezra 8.9 King James Version of Bible. Unless otherwise stated all Bible references are from the New International Version (International Bible Society).

Chapter 2:

From the inside looking out

The story of the beginnings of Providence House have been told better than I can tell it here, in Elizabeth Braund's book, 'The Young Woman Who Lived in a Shoe'. By the time I arrived in 1973 the great urban social revolution was well underway. The old streets of terraced housing behind Clapham Junction, that surrounded the old Providence Chapel had been swept way. The Winstanley Estate had been built for a number of years. York Road II estate with its housing blocks as long as a small street was opened, as was York Road 1 estate, with the winding complex of Badric Court, and the Totteridge Tower. It was while I had been at Providence for some years, that the rest of the old housing off Falcon Road was cleared and the Kambala Estate built, followed by some smaller housing areas. The new Providence House youth club was officially opened in March 1970, in a prominent location along Falcon Road, a hundred yards from the great Clapham Junction railway bridge, and a contrast to the old Baptist chapel, hidden way in the now vanished junction of Speke and Winstanley Road. It was built almost as an add on to the new Livingstone Estate, sharing an access pathway behind our building, and sharing a common row of shops across the passageway: a grocer and green grocer, a betting office and laundrette, and of course a fish and chip shop, perhaps prophetically named, The Bosphorus, given the transnational way the area would develop in later years.

When I arrived in the area the old character of the neighbourhood was already rapidly changing, and the cultural and ethnic diversity that has continued to this day was making its impact in the community. I can remember my early days in Providence House and the baptism into a vibrant and varied youth club and mission, a stranger to London, to housing estate life, to a very mixed community, and being a young man, learning every day.

From the outset the experience of Providence House was amazing. My daily tasks began, after I had clocked off from Woolworths at 1pm, until the last person left the building, and the last sweepings of the broom had been scooped up at night. Apart from a locally managed playgroup every morning, all that took place in this two-storey detached building was the active work of Providence House. A ground floor with a reception coffee bar and small kitchen, a small office and my 'cupboard' behind. A central club room on two levels, with an arts or table tennis room off one side and snooker room off the other. A staircase led to a first-floor sports hall about the size of a basketball court, with tall folding doors opening onto a stage, also known as the chapel.

The sports hall, cold in the winter, humid in the summer, was heaving every week with boys, mainly, playing non-stop football, from three and four a side to ten or twenty a side. So crowded you could barely find room to play the ball; yet those with high skill levels honed their cage ball talents. If you speak with those who were boys then, as I do often at funerals, the first thing they might talk about was the 'murder' ball in the hall. When I talked with Michail Antonio, of West Ham United, as part of a Sky TV programme in 2022, he spoke with fondness of that little sports hall, where he grounded his quick foot skills in continuous small sided games, and where he developed that sense of balance, and hunger and enthusiasm, that proved so crucial to his professional career, and to that of many other young men.

The sports hall also heaved with people every Friday night for the reggae dance. More of that later. At times it was so full there was room only for young men and women to stand as statues.

Good job the reggae of those days was slow rhythm rather than disco fever.

Monday nights were quiet nights, with a handful of young people coming in for particular things. I was asked to run a small football group, and I recall among others Glenroy Gottshalk and Philip Dillingham coming in to practice. They were tall even then, and as adults they tower towards six-foot six inches. I remember for a while trying to teach a young Jamaican lad called Roy to read, but not for long enough to make a real impact.

Tuesdays were junior nights, with over 70 boys and girls, and at its height topping 90. Black and white, all full of energy; ball games, art and craft, team games, tuck shop and Miss Braund's famous Bible stories. A tradition I continued after the farm project started, and eventually finding my own voice and own way of telling the story, with the aid of mojo sweets and lollipops to aid behaviour management. I think what I learned from listening and doing was the richness of Bible stories to resonate with our lives, how to get behind the colour of the stories without adding pointless information, such as making up names for Bible characters when we are not given them, and letting the power of the story speak. It was always the power of the story. The moment you thought you could add a neat application at the end to sum up the purpose of the narrative, was the moment you lost them, and the moment you literally saw their eyes ease away from the earnestness of attention. The trick was to convey the message during the story. If you think about it, that's what the Bible does. The stories are strong on simple narrative and short on detailed moralising. And, of course, I learned this, that that child who appeared to be hardly paying attention, actually knew the answer to the questions. It still surprises me.

The club ran from six to eight pm for most of my years, but in recent times we have replaced it with two highly successful after school afternoon clubs for juniors. I passed on that baton a while ago.

Tuesdays didn't end at 8pm in the early days, because after the club some of the men from the old Providence came to run their own football session. In those days the gents' toilet had a small shower they could use. One or two of these men were still in touch at the Providence House 50th anniversary that we held in 2014.

In those first few years everyone was untrained. Elizabeth and Rosemary were very experienced and embedded in the community. A sports coach would come on a Thursday, and Fred, a local window cleaner came in on Wednesdays, he being a well-known local goalkeeper and parent. All the helpers were volunteers and most came from Westminster Chapel, from where they knew Elizabeth. What they had was a willingness and a faith, which I guess would go along well with any organisation.

One gentle helper was Jim Clark, a resourceful stalwart in all things building related, and who tirelessly maintained the premises and improved it where the original designs fell victim to the everyday wear and tear of energetic young people; but Jim didn't really have the people savvy for youth work. One Wednesday, in the early days when I had taken the reins in the club, the television went missing. A couple of the lads simply unplugged it and picked it up from the coffee bar and walked out through the front door. Jim was minding the door. It was a few minutes before I was alerted by a frantic volunteer. I asked Jim whether he had seen anyone carry out the TV. He said yes, but didn't think anything of it, and no, he didn't recognise any of the young people. I managed to ascertain that a youth known as Pagan was if not one of them certainly knew who it was. Following Elizabeth's remote instructions from Dartmoor, I went to his family home, spoke with an older brother Frank, and said that if he couldn't locate and arrange the return of the television, then the dance wouldn't take place on Friday. Duly with half an hour to go, Kenny Reid came into the club his arms enveloping the abducted television. It was only a black and white TV, but it was all we had, and it belonged to Rosemary. In those days of the seventies the young people would huddle around it to watch Top of the Pops, and other community attractive shows. Things have moved on from then.

In those days all the volunteers were not formally trained. That was true also for me. I confess that in almost all the years in harness, I hardly undertook any youth work training; but I do think I learned at the hands of a master, Elizabeth Braund, in her perhaps unusual, unorthodox methods. I learned, too, at the hands of experience. The wisdom came with experience, and I believe with the providential guidance of God.

There is a lot of talk these days about 'lived experience', which I suspect is not as cut and dried as at times it is made out to be. I found quite soon after being landed with the responsibility of leadership, that I needed the support of volunteers with embedded experience, who had grown up in the housing estates, who were part of the culture. They brought with them that knowingness, that ability to anticipate before something went wrong. The best of them bought into the ethos of Providence House. They loved the place as their own. That was worth more than a dozen workers, paid to be a part of the service.

I can recall in 1981 on the second night of the inner-city riots, when Clapham Junction was still feverish with pockets of disorder, as I looked out of the first-floor window of Providence watching Redman walk across the car park and peer into the front of Providence. I later asked him what he was doing, and he replied, "Making sure that the building was safe" – even though all around were smashed and looted shop fronts.

I can remember in the first decade of the millennium during a warm summer's evening, when young people were milling around

22

on the forecourt, including one or two young people who didn't regularly attend. All of a sudden, a couple of vehicles swung into the car park. Out came some young men, who had a grievance with one of these occasional attenders and were intent on carrying it out there and then. The antennae of our helpers tuned into red alert. I can remember Jermaine quick as a flash putting a firm hand against the pocket of one of these men, to prevent whatever weapon was lurking in there ready to come out. Fortunately, sense and equilibrium prevailed, the men disappeared, as did our occasional guest, with a scolding in his ear not to bring his misdemeanours to our door again.

I am not sure if I could have survived those decades of the late seventies and eighties without that kind of support, at least in the clubs for teenagers, rather than in the junior work, where it was and always is easier. After that, my own experience and, dare I say it, my own stature in the community of Providence and the wider community carried a bit of weight. The downside of these local volunteers is that while they could share the love of Providence, they were not able to share the love and faith of Christ. They hadn't yet reached that point in their journey.

I wonder, looking back, if I had had a more enterprising, God-trusting faith, whether both qualities would have fallen into place: experience of the lived community and the natural awareness that it brought, and an experience of Christ, as real life, real faith saviour for a downtown housing estate. Truth is, I found that too often the church didn't get what went on in these communities, or if it did then church was for them a way out of the rawness of the life on the edges. I remember talking with a mother, probably around 2015, outside Providence House. She had two teenage children, both of whom attended our clubs. Her son was a lively lad, and never very far from getting into trouble with the wrong sort. She was waiting for one of them to leave for a weekend trip to the farm. I told her they would arrive back about 8pm on Sunday night, in case she wanted to collect them. She said she wouldn't have returned from church by then, and explained it took most of the day. A couple of buses, the service, the after service, the food, the two buses home, but clearly it was important to her. It was a space away from all the madness of Surrey Lane housing estate, where they lived. I was glad that church, and hopefully Christ, gave her respite, but was not surprised that her son was more and more away from her influence. Some months later police raided her house, because her son was using it as a drug distribution centre, and how much did she know or not know about that.

However, I remain indebted to all those volunteers, who embraced the ethos and value of Providence House, those from supporting churches, Westminster Chapel, Ashford Congregational, Westcliff Baptist, the Free Church of Scotland at Cole Abbey, St Stephen's. Careforce, whose young men, lived in the Providence flat, and laboured and wearied and prayed with a cheerful face. The London City Mission whose summer volunteers provided the backbone of helpers in the holiday clubs in the eighties and spilling into the nineties. To those from the local community, who grew up in Providence, and gave back as they could. I will name only a sample, who represent so many more, which space prevents from mentioning; but you know who you are, and the part you played. For now, to mention Lloyd Richards, Gillian, Redman, Sabu, Derek and Joe, Aston and Raymond, CB & Jerry, Terry Houston, from the early decades, and the A team of Floyd, Andrew, Wilson, Seon, Leon, Bernard, Michael Maloney, and Jamel Harding, that took us into the new century.

I am grateful most to God, that in the midst of every up and down, the times when we seemed too few to operate, or had too little to operate with, that there always 'sufficient for the day'. To probably misquote Jesus, at the last supper, when the disciples showed to him that they only had two swords to prepare against what lay ahead, he said: 'That is enough.' (Luke 22.38). I have always found there to be enough.

Wednesday nights at Providence in my first years, however, were the nights. So different from today, sometimes I wonder how it was managed. Elizabeth was at the front door, dour, matriarchal, a leather bag in her arm to keep whatever in it, and an old orange marmalade tin in which to collect the subs. Three pence when I started, and gradually growing with inflation to 5p, 20p, 50p and a £1 or £2 today. I think that Elizabeth was the best of all of us at collecting the money, but I carried it on until my retirement as a youth worker. It was a principle.

From 6.30-8.30 about 60 boys and girls, more boys than girls, 11-14 years old, came in using every part of the building. Then from 8.30-10.30, my first real introduction to London Caribbean culture and about 100 to 150 young black, mostly male, noisy, assertive. Table football, table tennis, a version of pool on the snooker table, youth filling every corner, and the almost twenty-a-side football in the sports hall. It was some atmosphere. Thursday nights and more young people of school age. Then Friday nights was the sound system, and when I first arrived the Danny King sound, and young adults from all over London, flocking into the space, to hear their music, find their own identity, their own cultural sounds in the city. Saturdays were football. At its height in the late seventies there were seven teams and I have no idea how we managed to run them. Towards the end of the nineties, we were more organised, better trained, and with more ambition.

Sunday was always the Lord's Day. Seventy or more children each week. The day the numbers slipped below fifty at some point in the late eighties, I felt that something was perhaps slipping away in my hands. Each week some of the children would be collected in the minibus. The same thing happened on a Tuesday evening. Over the years we have had different collection routes, often two or more loads of passengers. The old green-blue Bedford used to be seen along behind Battersea High Street and up Lavender Hill. The orange Ford Transit, that we bought for £1 from insurers, ran along Shuttleworth Road and then the streets off the Northcote. The blue bus, donated one Sunday by Westminster Chapel, that we called the Spaceship, ferried children from the Maysoule Road estates, and beyond, near Wandsworth roundabout. The white Transit, another gift, and of which a rear wheel fell off on one outing, served us well in going about the neighbourhood. Not to forget the blue ex-Navy Sherpa, that eventually gave up its ghost after being run ragged back and forth from Dartmoor; or the brand-new Ford Transit, purchased with a local authority grant, and the jewel in our crown, until someone else wanted it as their jewel, and early one morning stole it from under the windows of Providence House. We have operated since then with locally rented buses, although we ceased regular collecting of children some years ago, as indeed we finally ceased our Sunday School work, in 2015.

Not everyone who attended Providence House attended Sunday school, although many had opportunity to listen to Bible stories in Providence, or at the farm, or in this twenty first century to pop into Sunday First. There were those in truth who attended the youth clubs, the Friday nights, joined the Saturday football teams, who never entered our doors on Sundays; but Sundays at Providence brought hundreds of young people into contact with the Christian message, who might never had done so otherwise.

When I first came here, Elizabeth Braund said to me that the white working-class children who come to Providence know next to nothing about the Christian faith. The white kids if they are Irish and Catholic know a bit, but the West Indian children come with a background of Bible knowledge. Even that has changed. It has changed because this generation to a large extent, who have followed on with the brought over faith background of their parents, has failed to grasp the value of gospel truth. Failed to grasp it and to let it change their lives, and which would have provided the one antidote to all the madness that has gone on our community: too many aimless young people, unaware of God in this world and following those without God paths, that lead only to more aimless destructive consequences.

Having said that, there is by 2023 a far more diverse faith background than there was when I started out, not the least of different faith groups, and no faith groups, of more diversity of Christian leadership and cultural worship styles at a time, when traditional approaches are finding it harder to hold their place. More significantly from my perspective in this particular neighbourhood right behind Clapham Junction station, there are half a dozen gospel led churches in this square half mile, again representing a diversity of leadership and congregation. And they have all been talking with each other. Only time will tell whether the talking continues and joint community outreach grows from it. There is an opportunity in this decade that I haven't seen in my previous five in this neighbourhood.

I wonder whether there will be the faith and commitment to realise the words of Zechariah the prophet, a witness himself to changing times, in a way of urban regeneration, though nothing like the scale we are witnessing. 'This is what the Almighty says: once again men and women of ripe old age will sit in the streets, each with cane in hand because of his age. The city streets will be filled with boys and girls playing there. In those days ten men from all languages and nations will take hold of one believer by the hem of his coat and say, let us go with you, because we have heard that God is with you.' (Zechariah 8).

Only time will tell.

Chapter 3:

Black inside

It didn't take long for a fight to break out. After all, the lads were in a different manor. After all, they were those kinds of kids, where a need to fight might not ever be far away.

It was the summer of 1974, and we were on a Holiday Club outing to Holland Park adventure playground. It had been a regular feature of Providence summer clubs. Rosemary was driving the minibus, because Elizabeth was away, as her elderly mother had had a fall in a care home. There was a second minibus, that Danny King, of sound system fame, was driving. The group of young people from Providence House were teenagers, both white and black. The white boys, mainly coming from Winstanley Estate, where they had a bit of a reputation. Winstanley in those days was more white than black, whereas the Livingstone Estate, behind Providence, was more black than white. It made for interesting social dynamics.

The white lads got into a fight with some Holland Park local boys, and it was a bit of thing to sort it out, to separate the combatants, and make a judicious retreat to the minibus, before things escalated. What still sticks in my mind was the comment of one of the fighting boys. When the rumpus broke out, the white boys expected the black boys would stand and watch, because it wasn't their fight; but no, they joined in, because it wasn't about colour at this point. It was about place. They were all from Battersea. It was that they commented on, with surprise that for that moment they could be brothers in arms. I am not sure who said the revealing words, but it could have been Timmy or Danny Lovesey, and I expect that among the black lads were Morris and Byron and Travis. It was a long time ago, but it taught me two things. One was that there was prejudice and difference and different expectations among those of different colour and culture; secondly, and most importantly, as you got to know people some of the stereotyping fell away, and to use a phrase of Elizabeth Braund, you began to see people as people. She would in her later years repeatedly use this phrase to get beyond seeing people in categories, or statistics, or as clients. By the way at Providence House, we never had clients – they were always members.

The racial thing was real in the seventies. Today it is still real, only it is covered up. Battersea in the twenty first century is a wonderful mixture of cultures, as most urban centres are, a cocktail of culture and language, of colour and demography; but look closely, and you may see that we live parallel lives. Look at the societies, look at the churches, look at the politics, go to funerals and weddings; by and large we live in parallel to each other, while often sharing the same space. I wonder if in this respect the church, in this country, across the board, missed a huge opportunity in the post war years, and in doing so failed to grasp the true gospel implication of the work of Christ on the cross, to break down the barriers between peoples; when they of all groups could have demonstrated that in Christ there is a true integration. But no, we preferred our parallel lives. There are, of course, exceptions.

For the young people pouring into Providence House in the seventies race was a real issue. It was a real issue for the white working-class young person, who had already had their old housing communities disrupted, and now they had to make a double adjustment into the new high-rise blocks of flats, coupled with living next door to the growing numbers of families of a different background. In addition, they had to share space in their youth club with growing numbers of youths of a different culture. Those families and young people who worked this out found their lives enriched by this new mixed society.

When I first started at Providence House in 1973, there was a serious attempt to hold all this together, to keep the young people from the traditional Battersea community involved and at the same time facilitate the newer cohort as comfortable members. Key to this where it worked were those Caribbean families whose children had attended the old chapel youth club, and had become embedded in the Battersea community; some of those still shine as beacons of integration today. Successful integration started with young people, who were able to bridge that gap between cultures, and could live as both black and white. Noel Mckoy and Derek Richardson as young black boys, and Stuart Beasley and Gary Flatt as young white boys stand out as positive catalysts.

There is no doubt that for the black youth in Battersea in those days they experienced racism, but significantly for us they found that at Providence House there was a place they were welcomed, and they found a place they could belong, and they found a place they could call theirs. In this respect Providence House, under Elizabeth's leadership, was ahead of its time. Under my leadership this concept continued to be the case. Over and again if you talk with men and women who grew up in this community, they will testify to that sense of belonging, nostalgically, proudly, earnestly.

There is no doubt that for many of the white youth in Battersea in those days they found integration to be a difficult thing. At Providence House in the seventies, the junior work was a very mixed-race affair. The majority of the youth work with older teenagers had already become a black majority set up with the older youth club and the dances. The intermediate age groups of eleven to fifteens was a healthy mixture – just about. I can remember Elizabeth commenting, that if one of the white youths enjoys what we do, he or she will bring a friend along; but if one of the black young people like what we do in the club, they will bring several friends along; and thus the youth club grew disproportionately black to white. It was an interesting phenomenon.

For better or worse, or for better and worse, the situation was resolved when in the late seventies a new youth club was opened. Due to the enterprise of the then vicar of St Peter's at the other end of the Winstanley Estate a new, locally funded youth club, and worship space, was established. Almost like the Pied Piper the majority of white boys migrated to the new Club 2000, leaving Providence House to become more and more a black identified youth provision. It wasn't as simple as that, because there remained a fair degree of young people crossing over between the two clubs; but it made a marker – that theirs was more the white end of the estate, and ours more the black end.

Time, of course, is a great healer, or perhaps more truly a blurrer of the lines.

I believe in providence. I believe in the providence of God, and maybe this was how it was all meant to happen, that Providence House was to be a place for all people – the sign on the old chapel declared 'All Welcome', and the modern logo of Providence is a house with the words 'Here for all' underneath, and underpinning it; but that Providence House was meant to be a place where a generation of Black British young people could find a place, could discover identity, could develop friendship – maybe that was meant to happen.

I can recall so many occasions in the youth club, at an event, in a sound system dance, at a funeral or celebration, being the only white person present, or almost the only white person present. Perhaps that, too, was part of the providence of God. It was Redman who would say that you're white on the outside, but black on the inside. I take it as a compliment, but I don't delude myself that I can stand in another's skin; but I do acknowledge that my life has been enriched by being a part of this community, accepted, belonging, even having leadership within it.

I didn't have a choice in where I was born. It was in Georgetown, (British) Guyana in December 1951. My father was a Congregational Church minister, and he had accepted an appointment to serve at Smith Memorial Church in Georgetown, bringing with him his wife and my mother Muriel, his own mother, my older siblings, Marian, John and Peter. I was born within twelve months of the family coming to Guyana, and my younger brother Andrew followed in late 1953; but not long after that my father having been struck with illness, the family had to return to England.

I have no memories of the land of my birth, just a split toenail as evidence, where as a toddler I bounced a full husked coconut on my tender feet, and the nail has ever since grown split. Perhaps the place of my birth has given me a sort of fellow feeling with Caribbean people who have filled the whole of my working life; and in my time I have gravitated as an honorary Guyanese to people who have featured in my life's journey here; such as Terry Houston who so successfully ran football teams with us in the eighties, Aubrey Silas, who is fond of returning and talking about Guyana and Providence, Pam Goodman, who has run the pupil referral unit at Providence House for several years and refers to herself as a 'lickle Guyanese girl', and Marlene Price, with whom I have worked in the Big Local project in the neighbourhood for over a decade.

Perhaps my birthplace is significant. Born in Smith Memorial Hospital, Brickdam, Georgetown, built in memory of John Smith, a British missionary martyred by the colonial authorities for standing alongside the enslaved communities. Perhaps the naturalness of Guyanese visitors coming to our house in Croydon in the late fifties paved the way for an openness of thinking in my developing mind.

Perhaps it was the providence of God at work giving me an open heart. Long may it continue.

There are a number of values or approaches or perhaps states of mind that have helped me along the way, and helped me to gain perspective in this work.

One is to accept people as they are. They are personal. They are people. They are not statistics. Everyone has some qualities. Even among the most notorious I have found some homely characteristics. That is not to say, we have not stopped people attending for a while, nor that we don't believe in change, because we most assuredly do. Possibly the greatest change is that people grow up, or grow out of certain ways. The tragedy is often leaving it too late.

There is the importance of opening windows in young people's lives. The standard term is 'widening horizons', and that is what we did. Holiday clubs, residentials to the farm, football teams, sailing trips.

There is the value of belonging to a place. This goes beyond how you view people. It is something about being part of their lives, part of the community, something about sticking around. This is not to say everyone should stay as long as I have stayed, but too often young people see professionals who come and go. They see impermanence, when what they want to encounter is familiarity. It is something of pride, that as one by one other youth clubs closed, we didn't; and that when the funding ceased in 2012 that somehow, we kept going.

Being here is a core value. Still being here is an enhanced core value. It is often hard to judge the value of youth work. Sometimes the unmeasured success is because of what didn't happen. Because a young person was with us, they didn't go out and do something they shouldn't have. The cliché that youth clubs keep young people off the street is not overused. Certainly not overused with us, because that is exactly what we did.

Going through a journey together, or being part of that journey, of being there to hear about the journey have proved invaluable.

It was August 1981. It was a Friday. There had been riots in a number of urban centres in UK. Would it happen in Battersea? As I walked along Falcon Road towards Clapham Junction, the sense of expectation was palpable. On my return I telephoned the local superintendent of police, to ask for advice on opening the Friday night dance, at which a large number of young people would be present. His advice was business as usual. His attitude might have changed a little, as later following a tip off, police with dogs came to search for the home-made explosives we were apparently making in the club. There were none. It was just a story.

Our Friday evening session carried on as usual, though probably with a sense of nervousness or anticipation. In those days, at one edge of our forecourt, we shared an adjoining brick wall with the Livingstone Estate. It was about 8 feet high, and with a bit of athleticism you could take a run at it, gain a foothold, and then clamber over the other side, where there was a concrete podium, that acted as a broad walkway onto the estate, with Bancroft House towering above it, and broad enough for us to play sport with young people on it. Underneath the podium was a covered car park, that also served in bad times as a criminal getaway avenue. What was important for this day was that from the podium, you could overlook the Providence House car park, and Falcon Road.

Closing time for the dance was 11pm, and there were two problems initially. A band of policemen were stood across the road from Providence, in riot gear, at the junction with Este Road. With hindsight I would say that was a poor strategy. There would have been other bands of police in other parts of the borough also. The other problem was that not all the youths from the dance wanted to go straight home; there was a curiosity to see how this would play out, combined with a desire to be part of something. This group gathered beyond our car park on the wide pavement in front of the grocers – now the Red Cross shop. There was no love lost between a mainly white police force and mainly black crowd of young men. There were also by this time groups of men gathered on the podium behind the wall, watching what was happening in the street below.

I am not sure how it started. I think one of the young men in the crowd by Providence threw a missile towards the police, and most likely those gathered on the podium hurled some more things. Then it all happened. Throwing and running, and police movements. Bizarrely, I and some of the volunteer leaders connected with the sound system did what we always did, sweep the car park of debris. While doing so, I was struck by a large stone on the shoulder aimed at a policeman standing near me. He asked if I was alright. I was, but a scar lingered for some weeks afterwards.

Meanwhile, we cleaned the car park, the sound system was dismantled and they packed away their van. There was a collection of girls still in the club, afraid to go home. I volunteered to take them in the minibus, and disappeared towards Lavender Hill, to leave Providence House locked up, the action on the streets to sort itself out. Half an hour or so later, I returned, having witnessed degrees of disorder at Clapham Junction. I parked the minibus, and assessed the situation. It appeared that there was continued missile throwing being conducted from the podium on the estate. I fatefully decided, I should have a look, and see if there was anyone there that I could reason with to desist.

I walked behind Providence House and along the sidewalk that rose up a ramp to the podium behind. In truth, apart from a strapping youth, known as Monkey Man, I think for his athletic versatility, I didn't recognise anyone. There didn't appear to be people from the Providence dance that I could see, but they may have been elsewhere in the neighbourhood. There were as many white as black faces, who felt they were ideally placed on their raised platform, with easy escape routes into the flats behind. Any remonstrations I might have made would have fallen on deaf ears.

I returned to Providence and entered by the side door to join my colleague Simon Carlton, who shared the flat with me. He had been a volunteer for a number of months. A short while later, there was a knock on the side door. It was Mark Rose. Mark was one of the white youths from Winstanley, who we knew well, and who was a regular visitor to the farm on Dartmoor. He said he had called to see if we were safe.

That may have been another fateful thing, because soon afterwards, there was loud banging at the side door. I went to answer it, followed by Mark. A couple of policemen were there, who grabbed me roughly and Mark. I noticed a female police officer, who had done some work in the community with us, standing, watching and saying nothing. We were taken to the police wagon, and thrown to the floor, at the feet of several police officers, who were told that 'if he raises his head, hit it'.

At the police station, the officer who had enquired about my shoulder outside Providence, was behind the desk, signing arrested persons in. He expressed surprise that I was there, but not a word about that I shouldn't have been there. I was beginning to learn that in this big 'gang' priorities and loyalties will always lie a certain way. What surprised me that night was the people who seemed to have been caught and arrested were, like us, people in the wrong place at the wrong time, including a couple of deaf lads; rather than the actual perpetrators.

It was a single night in a single cell, with fried egg for breakfast. A duty solicitor took my case, and the magistrate reluctantly granted bail the next morning. The aforementioned superintendent sent a message to ask if he could see me. I declined.

Not surprisingly, the next day I stayed mostly indoors, and certainly on that night, and Simon and I watched the goings on up and down the street from the safety of the flat window at Providence House. It was reported in the press that two youth workers had been arrested in connection with the riots in south London. The other came from Brixton and I never learned who he or she was. Suffice it to say that a solicitor from ILEA took up my case, and it was thrown out when it came for trial, not because of the justice of my cause, but because the arresting officer from the police hadn't appeared, and the magistrate was annoyed. The same happened to Mark, who had a different solicitor.

It was unnerving at the time, but not as unnerving as the experience so many young men have, either through their own fault, someone's fault, or bad luck. As my friend Tas quipped 'one night in a cell doesn't make you one of us!' It is not that I gained any street credit from it, but for those who knew, it showed that my journey in parts resonated with theirs. This has always been important, this going through a journey together, or being part of that journey, of being there to hear about the journey has proved invaluable.

Sound systems. I've tapped my feet and nodded my head to Danny King's sound. I've carried boxes for Sticksman Hi Fi and First Class sound, and even driven a van for them to some out of the way housing estate in north London. I've been at Providence with Kilowatt and Nasty Rockers, with Lord David and Sir Coxsone, with Sufferer, Sophisticated Gents, Sir Lloyd and Jah Shaka; and all those other sounds whose names I have probably forgotten, and even Highway Hi Fi.

And I've fallen off a ladder for them the night Billy Boyo came to perform, and Courtenay the cab man, before he was Courtenay the cab man, drove me and my bleeding leg to the old St James's hospital; all of which almost jeopardised my wedding as a result (but my lovely Susan was patient then as she has forever been).

But there was a serious side to all those Friday nights, and it was something about social benefit. Again credit to Elizabeth Braund for seeing this, and trusting in the first instance the group of young men, from the Danny King sound, to lead this project responsibly. In the first place it was about black young people being able to hear reggae music, which they would find hard to buy in the local record shops. It wasn't until later that the iconic work of the Dub Vendor store in Clapham Junction started. The sound nights were about finding a voice for young black men and women. It was about finding and expressing identity. It was about discovering and growing community.

What stood out about Danny King's sound is that his crew were all in a professional career or trade, which brought with it a sense of awareness and commitment, along with the legendary Eddie as the bouncer, with his immaculate pin striped suits, his Mohammed Ali-like physical presence, but firm, gentleness, a sort of power hidden beneath civility. When Danny's star waned, and a succession of short-term sound system engagements didn't quite take off, we turned to a local group of men, variously known as Sticksman, First Class and I Spy; local men, brought up among Providence, with a wish to see Providence safe and community minded.

The music inspired more music. A group of boys from the youth club asked to use the hall to practise their dance moves and songs. They became known as The Pasadenas and achieved a UK number 5 hit with their tribute song, 'Right On'. Another group of budding musicians would arrive after school and practice on stage. In those days they called themselves The Albions, and most went on to have musical careers, Noel Mckoy in particular becoming an internationally known soul singer. Often when you read a summary blog about Wandsworth in the press, So Solid Crew, the hip hop collective, are mentioned. What could have been mentioned is that the key members came to Providence House, to the youth club, to the dances, some even playing in the football teams. All of which is an indicator of a rich artistic heritage that connects to Providence House.

As with so many things we did at Providence House, there was a risk involved. We had to weigh the risks against the benefits. Usually, Providence took the risk and the young people and young adults reaped the benefits, unaware there may have been a possible downside for us.

There was a social risk that came with large numbers of young people leaving the building at the same time, and cramming onto buses, or annoyed that buses wouldn't stop for them. I once attended a meeting of police and London Transport representatives about how to manage these journeys. There was the risk to reputation, that seeing a crowd of youths on the street on a Friday night, made local people walk onto the other side of the road, or not want to walk past. Yet inside the building it was extraordinary that so many lively young adults could be present and there be so little trouble. That was a striking feature also of the youth clubs, that sense of self-regulation, or of older young people monitoring the behaviour of young ones, when they might flare up. I consciously noticed this disappear in the nineties.

There was the risk that people would think we were just one thing: a Friday dance, because that was what they noticed passing by, or heard about on the grapevine. Meanwhile fifty children attending Sunday school, or a hundred boys in small groups on a Saturday for football, or regular minibuses driving off to the farm, went by unnoticed, because it didn't cause a stir. We took that because we stood alongside those young people in their journeys.

There was a different risk. I always hear stories of young people, young men or young women, who were not allowed to come; but come they did, by sneaking out of their houses, because they wanted to be at the dance. I suppose that has always gone on.

We were thankful that drugs were not an issue, or rather that we had ceased running sounds when smoking cannabis was added to by stronger substances. From the beginning, from our organising viewpoint keeping a handle on the smoking was not always easy. It became easier in later years, when all smoking inside a public building was forbidden; but before that it was hard. It was one thing to ask someone to put out a smoke, but we also had to contend with those who wanted to sell it.

When we finally let the sounds go, they had run their course. They had reached a natural conclusion as far as we were concerned, and it was also time for us to move on. The times were changing.

Without doubt I have some regrets. Regret that while for many the friendships they made at Providence led them to richer lives, for others it led them to choices, and it could be argued they made wrong choices. Regret that while out of the many layered associations in Providence has emerged some excellent community leadership, there has not at times been enough leadership within this community to show the next generation the way through, and to misquote a Bible phrase the sins of one generation have been visited on another. That is a social comment. Regret that although we have achieved diversity in Providence House, we never truly made a multi-racial youth club out of it. Perhaps that was always going to be hard.

I have an abiding memory. We used to take minibus, even coach, outings, in the eighties to Oxshott Woods, off the A3, and down a lane with multi-million pound houses on the one side, and the woods on the other. It was just what appeared be a countryside space to let loose some city kids, to run about, climb trees, and play games. One game we used to play was 'chain he'. I had learned it as a boy. There were probably thirty children in a grassy meadow, and one person was 'it'. His or her job was to catch someone, and hold their hand and become a chain. Very quickly the caught people were making up a chain of five, and more. When the chain became too unwieldy you could split into smaller chains. The chains kept chasing and closing in until everyone had been caught. The photograph that I took shows about six children ages 9-12. One of them is PJ Hanrahan, of Irish background who lived in Scholey House on Ingrave Steet. Another is Festus Ogwuda, of Nigerian extraction who lived on the Kambala Estate, and before that probably on the Livingstone Estate, but who sadly died before his time. I loved the photograph because it was black and white children of different backgrounds, playing together, holding hands. It was what I wanted to see, and to see grow.

There were things we never got to succeed with. Of course, there were; but there are things that without question we did achieve, together, and built a sense of belonging, and community, which is what Providence is all about. For that sense of belonging, I have no regrets.

Chapter 4:

Should I fall behind:

It was a Sunday afternoon, and I was getting the building ready for Sunday School. There would be around fifty children, some of whom I would collect in the minibus, some were brought by parents, some came on their own. It was the Spring of 1980.

A number of regular helpers came from the Congregational church in Ashford, Middlesex. These young enthusiasts jumped on the train and would join us for Sundays, for Tuesday junior clubs, sometimes for other youth clubs, and to help during the summer holiday. One such was a teenage Ian Smith, who returned at some point in his twenties to help with the annual accounts, then to become treasurer, and finally chair of trustees, and as of 2023 he is still heading up the trust, more years later than he would probably wish to remember.

On that particular Sunday, a school teacher, named Sue Poyle, who I had known from Heathfield days led the youngest children's group. She arrived that afternoon bringing with her a new helper or possibly just a visitor. This lady had only recently become a Christian, and was very eager, and had attended the church the previous Sunday for her first time, and been invited by Sue to have lunch at her house. On learning that she was off to this odd place near Clapham Junction, the visitor asked if she could come along the next week. Her name was also Susan, and the rest is sort of history.

Apparently her first look at me in the front room at Providence House gave her the impression that I was a bit on the short side. It appears, however, that in other ways I must have gained stature in her eyes, because an odd courtship that didn't look like a courtship took place. Susan being invited to help at a swimming gala, or a girls' outing to Birdworld in Surrey, or to the caves at Chislehurst with another group. In a clumsy way these encounters seemed to constitute a date. At possibly the first dining out together I recall falling asleep in the restaurant in Richmond, in what must have seemed to be a flawed expression of romance. Richmond was quite handy as I could drive there by Providence minibus and she by her small green Renault from Ashford.

I can remember going to visit Susan in her flat in Ashford and driving back listening to reports of the Falklands War on my car radio. I can remember on Fridays, going to see her at her workplace for the Church Mission Society on Waterloo Road, and having lunch together at the canteen of the Young Vic, then driving back across south London in my orange Ford Fiesta to Elliott School, in Putney, where I played five a side football for a number of years with school teachers. After which it was back to Providence House to get ready for the dance in the evening.

Somehow the fire kindled and that providential encounter in 1980 led to marriage in May 1983. Mind you, I almost fluffed it eight days before the wedding when a collapsing ladder at Providence fell, from which I was undertaking the regular Friday ritual of hooking 8 x 4-foot boards against the windows, as an amateurish sound barrier. My leg was ripped open, and I still have the scars to tell; and I was only released from hospital with 2 clear days to go before the wedding, and a wooden stick to accompany Susan and me up the aisle.

In 2023 it will be forty years together, and Susan has given far more than I can truly appreciate, or have ever really matched. In the old youth work terminology, there are three recorded and accredited outcomes, Joy, Mark and Rosie. Joy arrived just before the start of a week of outreach activities at Providence House in May 1984; Mark came just before the first of many Providence families' weekends to the farm in June 1986, and trying to be both at the bedside and leading the farm weekend was always going to be unsatisfactory. Rosie was born in the snow in April 1989. I was at Providence House, where the girls' indoor hockey team were practising, when Susan gave me the call. Close the club, drive home to Balham, take Susan to St Georges. In truth there was very little snow, but Rosie was a lovely baby.

Joy is a teacher, married to Tom, a structural engineer, with Elicia and Manny as children. Mark is a lead ranger for the National Trust and is married to Helen, a gardener. Rosie is a freelance writer and speaker and homemaker, and married to Woody, who is a Church of England minister, and Lily Grace is their daughter.

In some ways working in Providence is like being married, and by that I don't mean the same as Susan was warned, that if she married me, she would be marrying Providence House; which in effect she has done, thank the Lord, while at the same time pursuing a successful career as a teacher, a church children and families' worker, and a brilliant mother. What I meant is that both marriage and working at Providence are about commitment, about promise making and promise keeping. They are about keeping on, and keeping on keeping on. Both have been true in my experience of marriage and of Providence House.

To both also I could apply these words from Bruce Springsteen: 'We'd said we'd walk together come what may; that come the twilight should we lose our way, if as we're walking a hand should slip free, I'll wait for you; should I fall behind, wait for me.'

I could probably say these words, too, from Willie Nelson: 'Little things I should have said and done, I never took the time: you were always on my mind. You were always on my mind.'

I would definitely want these words remembered, that I wrote on a piece of paper and slipped into Susan's Bible, before she boarded an aeroplane to east Africa in the autumn of 1982, and that subsequently have repeatedly rung true: 'Blest be the tie that binds our hearts in Christian love; the fellowship of kindred minds is like to that above.'

Which brings me on to another sense in which being involved in Providence House is like a marriage: in that Providence is a family, and to many people it has been family. To some it has been a brother or sister, a parent or an uncle. A friend.

I think that is why our **summer holiday clubs** were so important, because in some ways they were about being family. They were already being run by Elizabeth and her team for three weeks every school summer holidays when I arrived, and we kept them going in some fashion or other, and still do so today. In fact, possibly almost without a break Providence House has organised summer holiday clubs for children since 1970 until the present time. That must be some kind of record.

I think we ran at Providence House the best children's holiday clubs in the London borough of Wandsworth. Summer after summer, hundreds of children, amazing committed volunteers, through the 1970s, through the 1980s, through the 1990s, and into this century. Always opening horizons, always opening new doors, always for everyone. Children, who have giggled and shouted their way through happy summers at Providence House. From the days of the seventies to the mid-eighties when kids almost fell out of the estate to run into Providence, from the Livingstone Estate, and Winstanley, and York Road and Kambala Estates. For so many of them it was the best of times, the time of their lives. A change in local funding and local regulations caused a change in the approach we could offer, but we have kept it going.

For years we provided a cooked meal, which in later times changed to bring your own packed lunch. Art and craft, drama, table tennis, pool and bar football, football and other sports. We followed a theme, with a Bible message, which we presented daily as a serialised story. Every afternoon outings, by bus or minibus or coach. To museums, to every public park, to the seaside. For a number of years, the council hired a train to the seaside, and we would book seats on it. I can remember 80 seats to Margate, and children with helpers on the beach and in the funfair, and counting the numbers on and off all day, and at the end, ready to leave for the train station. 77,78,79. Where was number 80? I cannot remember her name, but she lived on Pountney Road, off Lavender Hill, Battersea. No choice but to send the others ahead, and go, like the shepherd to find my lost sheep. Eventually she ended up at the police station, and we found a later train and got home safely. No mobile phones for keeping in contact in those days.

In addition to the day time activities, once the farm project had started, there would be summer residentials to Dartmoor, and again almost every single summer since 1976, Providence House has organised a residential for young people to the farm, for the first year at Bag Park Manor, and then for every year, except for a mere handful, there have been summer trips to East Shallowford Farm; that too must be some kind of record.

There is another story that appears to me as providence, or a God-incidence. The summer of 1980 to my best recollection. The summer club was busy. There were activities going on in every corner of the building, and Malcolm Hunter appeared at the doorway. He had contacts through his parents to the church in Ashford. I assumed he was another volunteer turning up, so without any real introduction asked him to help with the clay modelling in the coffee bar. That hadn't been Malcolm's plan. In fact, he didn't have a plan. He had given a friend a lift to Russell Motors, the motorcycle shop across the road from Providence

House, and as he stood in the doorway of the shop he looked around and saw the Providence sign over the porch, and wandered over, because his mother had told him about us.

After the club had finished, we talked. He was not in fact part of the cohort of young volunteers from Ashford. He was a carpenter, at that time living in a 'squat' in Tooting. He was also a keen fisherman and was to become a keen Christian, always ready to share his faith, his gifts, his energy and his life with others. His being a carpenter met a need they had on the farm that very month, and he joined another young man, Andrew Sloan, loosely connected to Providence House, via Westminster Chapel, who then went onto fill various volunteer roles at Providence and East Shallowford, from building advisor to a long serving trustee.

After that initial visit to the farm, Malcolm returned spending most of that summer and the next at East Shallowford, and came to live at Providence for several years, and worked at Providence in the end for eighteen years. Malcolm gave up his small business as a carpenter and started a training project for young men in the club. He would take lads who were out of school or out of work, seek out construction projects at local churches or charities or private houses and train the young people up in carpentry and building related skills. Some like Mark Hanrahan, Clive McDermott, Aubrey Silas and most notably Phil Dorman made a career out of carpentry. Working with Malcolm redeemed Phil's life in more ways than one, and currently six children and two marriages later he leads projects of Providence young adults to the farm, has become a trustee, and is on a vibrant faith journey.

There were those who gained a taste for work from Malcolm's carpentry project and went on to work at other things. There were those who didn't seem to get beyond just tasting what work looked like. All were exposed to an inspirational approach to life and work and faith. There was a time when most of the building improvements at both Providence and East Shallowford were the handiwork of Malcolm and his teams or of those who inherited his mantle. Having lived in Plymouth with his wife Elizabeth and two children since 1998, Malcolm has served time as a trustee at both Providence and Shallowford.

Malcolm got paid for working at Providence, or rather significantly under paid. I was adequately salaried by the local authority. It wasn't until the nineties that we started to access local authority funding to support sessional youth workers. Everyone else was a volunteer. Elizabeth Braund and Rosemary Bird were self-supporting, the latter working in the neighbourhood St John's hospital part time. Without the team of volunteers little effective work could have been done. Space prohibits the long list of volunteers who caught the vision and shared of their lives.

In one sense Doris gave her life. Doris Walters was from the nursing profession and had served with a Christian mission, European Missionary Fellowship, in Europe, since shortly after the second world war. She was now on her last posting, at the mission's student training home before retirement; but she helped twice a week at Providence. When the farm project started so suddenly in autumn 1975, and Elizabeth had asked me to keep things going, she knew I would struggle without older wiser help. Elizabeth persuaded the mission to second Doris to Providence House.

Doris was a small, round lady with silver hair, a sweet smile and a soft Welsh accent. On Sundays she helped run the Sunday School, Tuesdays the junior clubs, Wednesdays and Fridays ran the canteen amidst all the noise and roughness of those hectic nights, and she ran the elderly ladies group one afternoon a week. She had worked in refugee camps in Austria, so I don't think Providence phased her; but she got ill, and had to go away, and never recovered from her illness. That must have been 1978. I always wondered how Providence might have been had she had more time, more time to be there, more time to be an influence. That in itself may have been another providence.

After Doris, came Simon Carlton, a young enthusiast from Ashford, who shared with me the turbulent days of the early 1980s, before moving on to a career in nursing. After Simon came Dele or Ayodele Martin, who came from Westcliffe on Sea, another unsolicited providential contact. He lived with Malcolm and me at Providence, developed photography projects in the club, and moved onto a career in teaching. Others came and went, and made their mark, and to quote Bob Marley, 'good friends we had along the way.'

I will, however, go back to Bruce Springsteen for a quotation to end this chapter.

'Now everyone dreams of a love lasting and true, but you and I know what this world can do; so let's make our steps clear, that the other may see; and I'll wait for you – if I should fall behind, wait for me.'

Chapter 5:

Where the tree falls

Danny Lovesey and his mate were sitting by the lake fishing. I sat with them but didn't really know a roach from a reed. It was at Ashburnham Place, a former manorial house, but then a Christian conference centre. It was 1974. We were with a Providence House group staying in the rough and ready Save the Children Fund campsite in Burwash Common, a few miles away. Elizabeth Braund had contacts with the owners of Ashburnham, as she always seemed to have with the most unusual places for Battersea kids, and had secured permission for an outing to Ashburnham and its extensive grounds.

I was deputed to go with a couple of lads while they fished in the lake. I have no memory whether they had any bites that afternoon. They had been fishing for a while, when along came a group of people, who were obviously attending a Christian conference in the big house, and were out for a walk. Spying our lads they engaged in conversation, and sought to turn it into a faith witness moment. One of these well-meaning people asked Danny whether he wanted to meet the Lord.

Danny as quick as anything said yes, and the conversation drifted on and then off, as did the group of Christians; but apart from that question I cannot remember anything else that was said in that faith witness moment. Then suddenly for Danny the penny dropped.

'Oh, I get it, he meant the Lord Awmighty! I thought he meant the Lord of the big 'ouse.'

Motivated by good intentions, but bound by cultural clichés of messaging, it would have taken a bit more than a casual conversation to have made an impact with this 15 year old lad. As Elizabeth wrote: "Most of us soon learnt that it was all too easy to imagine that we were conveying some thought, when in fact the children understood something different from what we had said, or understood nothing at all." [*1] That was a principle I learned early on in my time at Providence House, and we have had to keep learning ever since. It may seem obvious but it never is, that **communication must be understood and be on the wavelength of the hearer**, and not camouflaged by culture, even Christian culture.

Providence House is an independent evangelical Christian charity that has been working among families and children and young people in the housing areas north of Clapham Junction, Battersea, since before 1963. It is not a story about revival, but it is about some lives renewed, many lives signposted, and witness given. Its work is not a blueprint example for successful mission, but it is an example of perseverance, of engagement, of taking on challenges, of finding a path and sticking to it. It is essentially a local story of believing people, of making connections, and a faithful God. It is a story about discovering principles and values that work and applying them, and keeping to them. This chapter endeavours to illustrate some of them.

The story of Providence House begins with a woman who read the Bible – where else should it start? But she didn't read it because she wanted to, but because she was paid to. In fact, she wasn't paid to read it in the first place, but to research the history of how the Bible came into the English language, and the lives of those who made it happen. Already a script writer for the BBC, she was asked to research and script a series of radio programmes in the 1950s on the story of the English Bible. She didn't want to do it, because she wasn't a Bible reading, church going person. Friends pressed her to do it, and she embarked on a journey of discovery, via the tales of brave men and women who suffered to bring the Bible into the native language, via believing friends and God moments, and finally to personal faith in Christ.

Encouraged to combine her writing ability with her fervent faith, she started a magazine called the Evangelical Magazine. Beginning in 1959, the administration of the magazine soon outgrew her Kensington flat, and following a tip off and sitting on a No 49 bus, she landed in Battersea, and to a empty Strict Baptist Church, called Providence Chapel, in an area of row after row of Victorian terraced houses, regularly interspersed with damaged areas, still unhealed from wartime bombing.

And here is the first principle for those thinking about Christian mission, about church mission, probably any mission, and indeed for life's journey. **We need to be ready for the unexpected, we need to understand that our plans only take us so far**: The Book of Proverbs states, that 'in his heart a man plans his course, but the Lord determines his steps.' (Proverbs 16.9).

Elizabeth Braund made her plans, organised the old vestry into an office, and the school hall for bi-monthly packing of magazines for posting, and got on with the work in less than standard premises, with the lean-to kitchen with one cold tap and leaking roof, the outside toilet adjacent to the flooded cellar, and meeting the occasional rat on the way. But what she hadn't bargained for was local curiosity, for people stopping her in the street. Nor was it a part of her editorial plans for a serious Christian periodical, that she should take any notice of the countless people unconnected with any church, or with the kids that played on the streets and in and out of the bomb sites.

Not being a children's worker, she arranged for those apparently more experienced to try and revive the Sunday School, and visit the houses. Not being used to running ladies' Bible meetings she arranged for people to run them in the chapel. And so unintentionally she became drawn into something more than she first planned. Then something happened to change all that. It was a late afternoon probably in 1961, and an invited guest was addressing a handful of elderly women, and Elizabeth was seated alongside them …

The few women sat huddled at the end of the forms nearest to an oil stove which disgorged fumes and a little heat. The speaker had chosen as his text 'One there is that sticketh closer than a brother', and his discourse was designed primarily to encourage the sixty to eighty-year-old age group. Suddenly, the street door burst open, there were giggles and scuffles, a ball bounced on the floor, and someone protesting loudly was shoved in to collect it, while grinning faces framed the door. Obviously, Elizabeth had not been paying close attention to the discourse, for she moved quicker than the small boy and was at the door before he was able to recapture the ball and make his escape.

'Come on in everyone,' she invited. This response was evidently so unexpected that it made the boys stand stock still. They shuffled in embarrassed and she sat down with them, the ball in her hands, on the bench at the back, 'We're having a meeting,' it was explained, 'and you are quite welcome.' Somehow the meeting got to a thankful close. The boys moved smartly to the door, where they got their ball back and invitation to come to the afternoon Sunday-school. [2] She had little thought of seeing the boys again. Nevertheless, when she came down to the chapel next Sunday afternoon, they were all there, plus more. One of those boys was Les Tucker, who kept in touch with Providence House throughout his life, in between living a bit of a rough existence, and kept in touch almost to the end of his life. I conducted his funeral in 2012, and his grown-up daughter now invariably attends our Sunday First monthly meeting.

In one sense the rest of the work of Providence follows from that 'Can I have my ball back?' episode. This is a principle of mission that we need to be ready for the unexpected, we need to understand that our plans only take us so far.

There is an allied principle to the first one, and it is this: curiously enough **it is important to be in the place you think you should be, because there, God may lead you on**. Abraham's servant in Genesis 24.27 said, that 'I being in the way, the Lord led me.' Elizabeth Braund some years later wrote in a report to her trustees: "But God has never failed nor, in an extraordinary way, have we ever failed to have sufficient to do any work He has intended us to do – though often we have seemed at the outset to have nothing. It has proved to us beyond any doubt that the way is to go on – and as you go on you will be enabled." *[3]

Sunday by Sunday these street boys turned up, and then with older and younger brothers and sisters, and cousins and friends, and before long they asked this question: 'Can we 'ave a club Miss?'

Sometimes there are transcendent moments in mission, and this was one of them, because so much followed on from it, so much so that the magazine was eventually overtaken by the work of Providence House, and the writer became a youth worker, and eventually a farmer. The empty chapel became full again, with children and young people, with families, with the elderly; with people in crisis, with those who wouldn't go to a church, with those young people who wouldn't go to more organised youth centres, with young people falling into crime, or into drugs.

The magazine somehow managed to get published regularly throughout the sixties. Nobody was paid. Everyone was a volunteer. For those who came it was their place, their space, where they belonged, and affectionately they called it 'prawnies' because they could not quite roll the 'r' for Braund. Other churches for what they were, in the area, were not quite sure what to make of it. The local authority and youth service were initially curious, thinking it would blow away, and then took a greater interest realising that this work was positively affecting young people's lives. The Baptists wanted shot of the old building and in 1963 sold it to Elizabeth Braund and team, who renamed it Providence House and set up as a charity. The council wanted shot of pretty well everything, so lock stock and barrel, bit by bit, the whole area was flattened and out of the dust rose in turn one, two, three, four housing estates. Providence House itself came down in 1968-9, and a new building in a new location was opened in 1970.

We are still here today.

My next principle is that the Christian worker, or the effective youth and community worker, must be **embedded in the community** he or she serves. That was clearly the case for Elizabeth Braund and her colleague Rosemary Bird. It was shown at Elizabeth's funeral in 2013.

The men who carried the coffin at her funeral further illustrated something of the broad span of her influence over many years – Bob whose family knew Elizabeth from the very beginning of Providence House, and went on to become a master plasterer; Joe who recalls one long summer at Shallowford that made a big difference to his teenage development and his subsequent music career; Malcolm whose life of practical service to others was inspired by Elizabeth both at Providence House and the Farm; Jamel who from childhood to manhood has made the regular journey from Battersea to Widecombe year after year, and has developed from member to volunteer to staff member and is now pursuing a career in youth work in south London; Paul who was given the opportunity to farm at East Shallowford, and now has his own family farm and dry stone walling business; and Peter, who in some ways represents the past – his wife's family having known Elizabeth for three generations -

and the future, in that he became a trustee of the Shallowford Trust.
*4

In my own journey at Providence House, I found myself thrust into a large black Caribbean youth culture, and found myself one of them, as family, as brother. In 2014 we celebrated roughly 50 years of Providence, and in talking with people about the story, they kept repeating that it has been 'Part of our Lives'. We have since adopted it as a way of describing the work of Providence House.

I believe there is a credibility to the gospel, when the worker embeds him or herself in the community to live it out, and not just commute in with the message. That doesn't mean you have to stay in one place for 50 years! But it does require a sense of staying.

A similar or allied principle is what Providence House has as its strapline on its logo: 'Here for All'. Clearly in theory every church has that as a principle, but in practice the reality is far from the case. At Providence House we have to constantly refresh ourselves with this, and we have had debates about how far to take it. In the 1960s, Providence House entertained those who were called the unclubbable. In the transition days of the late 1960s they housed drug addicts. In the melting pot of the seventies, we gave space, their own space, to black youths before anyone else really did in Wandsworth. More often than not, the congregation for Sunday First seemed to attract those whose lives were a bit on the edge.

I would like to say that there should be an openness about the worker, open in heart and open in appearance and access. To borrow from a hymn: "There's a wideness in God's mercy, like the wideness of the sea...For the love of God is broader than the measure of man's mind, and the heart of the eternal is most wonderfully kind." These words from Frederick Faber, the hymn writer, naturally migrate from the character of God to the character of a Christian worker. Or they should. It is a measuring stick.

Elizabeth Braund stood out as a Christian thinker. I would like to think that this is a principle of a worker that there should be a **deeper perception from those in Christian mission than there is in society at large**, or even professionals in society. That there should be a willingness to think deeper, look more closely below the surface, to be discontent with easy answers. But it is not true enough. I wish it were more true of me. I wish it were more true of Providence House.

But Elizabeth Braund saw that something was missing. She along with her colleague Rosemary observed, that despite all the new facilities of the modern housing that transformed the streets around Clapham Junction, something had been lost, in terms of a sense of community and identity. She did not want to turn back the clock, but she did want to help restore some connections. She felt that there was something intrinsically negative about an entirely man-made concrete environment, divorced from the natural world that God had made. She felt that inner London was gasping for something. She wanted to find a Lung for the City. She felt she wanted a farm.

She thought and she talked, and she became convinced that she had to find a place, a permanent place that she could take young people to. She wanted it to be as different from London as possible, somewhere with a bit of wildness and challenge about it, somewhere with a sense of community to it, a working farm where children could learn and participate in nature. And so in 1975, she came to Dartmoor, and rented a property for a year in Widecombe in the Moor, and in the following year, providentially, East Shallowford was purchased.

And we've been farming ever since.

What you see happening here is a pioneer worker, embedded and trusted in the community she served, seeking to live and communicate the message of Jesus in words and actions that made sense to people; with one eye open to the community that she lived in, and another open to the Word of God, she was able to apply Christian thinking to social outcomes and make decisions based on both.

Wow! That is the sort of radical thinking we should all aspire to, rather than be content to let one year drift into another. Led by the hand of God, Elizabeth and Rosemary started something unique, and Providence has been going ever since.

Thus the work has continued. With youth, with families. In London, at the farm. Through Sunday Schools, through holiday clubs. Through peace and harmony, through riots. Through volunteers coming and going, through the death of the founders. Through new leaders, through changing leaders. Through wave after wave of demographic change.

But through trust, fixed and faltering, in an unchangeable God, and in His unchangeable word.

I wrote a short reflective book about Ecclesiastes in the Old Testament, and some of the metaphors there seemed to almost be talking about the work of Providence House

'Cast your bread upon the waters, for after many days you will find it again.' Ecclesiastes 11.1.

Funny that, as I would have thought it would have come back soggy, but maybe it is cornbread. The image in the writer of Ecclesiastes' mind is perhaps of a merchant who sends his corn by ship, and it must cross many waters before he ever knows what return it will get. But he doesn't hesitate to send it, to cast it. More importantly it is about not being stingy or reluctant to share or hesitant to do or speak or give.

I recall one night outside Providence House, a young man, Kyle, was telling a friend how that Providence had been an early

Christian influence on his life. And now some years later he has a good job, is married, is committed to his church, and for a while served as a youth pastor. The bread was cast upon the waters, and after many days it is found again. We do not know what a good word, a gift, a helpful action will lead to, or what effect the work we now do with a young person will have.

So spread it, cast it, share it, and leave the result to God.

Ecclesiastes also says, 'Give portions to seven, yes to eight, for you do not know what disaster may come upon the land.' (Ecclesiastes 11.2). Appropriate at any time a verse about giving, but it is not here talking about giving to your family, however big it is. It is about generosity; it is about giving to need. It is about giving as a life principle. You see a need, you give. You give something, you give your time, you give yourself. It is a mission principle. It is a youth worker's principle. It is a neighbour's principle. You give it to one, then there is another. There is no time when you say, I can do no more, I have given enough. I am going to shut the door. There is always one more.

That is the type of mission worker that is required. I wonder how Jesus ended his working day when one by one the people kept coming for help. To quote the old hymn - 'he giveth, and giveth, and giveth again.' To quote the prayer of Ignatius Loyola: 'to give and not to count the cost, to fight and not to heed the wound, to labour and not to ask for any reward, save that of knowing that we do thy will.' 'Give portions to seven, yes to eight.' It is also giving for the future. Giving is an investment in people's lives - 'for you do not know what .....may come upon the land.'

This is another principle that seems to fit: 'Whether a tree falls to the south or to the north, in the place where it falls, there will it lie.' (Ecclesiastes 11.3). Where God has placed you, that is where you have a work to do. Whether in a family, a place of work, a location, a community, he has placed you to be there for Him. We all get itchy feet at times. We want to be somewhere else. We think it might be better someplace else. St Paul wrote to Archippus who had itchy feet: 'See to it that you complete the work you have received in The Lord.' (Colossians 4.17).

I am not exactly sure who Archippus was, but I can remember one New Year, again in the early 1980s. I know it was then, because Simon Carlton was living at Providence House. I was beginning to think that I can't commit to another year at Providence House. Too many things, too many griefs, too many obstacles. When I read that verse, it was as if it was for me: continue or complete the work to which you have been called.

Matthew Henry, the Bible commentator, said: 'Everyone must labour to be a blessing in that place, whatever it is, where the providence of God cast him.' Ecclesiastes said, that whether a tree falls to the south or to the north, in the place where it falls, there will it lie. By the way - a fallen tree is a life source for a myriad of creatures, and keeps also the fire going. That is good to know. I knew where the tree lay for me.

There are more maxims from Ecclesiastes, but I will only mention them in passing.

'Whoever watches the wind will not plant; whoever looks at the clouds will not reap.' (Ecclesiastes 11.4). Ah, the fatal hesitancy, the immobility of doubt, the list of reasons why we cannot start - they all keep us from action, whether in life decisions, or mission, or whatever! As Carla Harris, a TED talk speaker has said, 'The price of inaction is greater than the cost of making a mistake.'

'Sow your seed in the morning, and at evening let not your hands be idle, for you do not know which will succeed, whether this or that, or whether both will do equally well.' (Ecclesiastes 11.6). There is a commitment here to action. Come on, get going, sow in the morning, sow in the evening, sow when you are young, sow also when you are older in the evening of your life. Sow! There is a commitment also to the adventure of trusting - you do not know which will succeed, and when.

There is an adventure of trusting in a work like Providence House, for you do not know which will succeed. To end this chapter with a story.

The phone rang. It was Brian. He was calling from the hospital. 'I don't think I have found Jesus, but I think he has found me.'

We never pushed Brian into faith, but we opened the door. Literally. It began when he brought his ten year old daughter to our holiday club at Providence House. Brian would often stay and have a cup of tea. He told us early on that he was not religious, but he kept in contact. We talked about cricket, about books, about our community work, a bit about faith.

He was not a well man. Excessive drinking and smoking had given him a respiratory and heart problem, which he seemed to manage. He was not always a happy man. He no longer lived with his wife. His daughter stayed for weekends, but they were getting less frequent. He was an intelligent man though, who had been around, done various things, and integrated well into a mixed-race community.

We invited him to our annual families' weekend to the farm. He got his prescriptions worked out, came well prepared, camped and blended in. I gave him the task of taking a photograph of everyone over the weekend. In fact, we still have a picture of him, sitting on the bench against the barn, Hawaiian shorts, broad rimmed hat, a roll up in his hand, smiling next to old Josey. He wasn't old, but life and habits had aged his appearance.

During the weekend one of the helpers on the farm said to us, 'there is a man who is searching for God.' We kept the door open for his search. He began to attend our Sunday meetings. He was direct. He would say if he could not believe something, but he wanted to get his head around what the Bible said. He would ask questions, go home and read the Bible for himself. And he kept coming.

During the summer holidays, perhaps 2006, we gave him another task to keep him with us. He would make sandwiches each day for the helpers. It may have seemed a little thing, but I can still recall Brian's spicy chicken and salad. He enjoyed the laughter and enjoyed the little enterprise. Week by week through the autumn he attended on Sundays. His gravelly voice added to our music. He valued the prayers that were made, especially during his first spell in hospital. During that stay he appeared to have panic attacks, and discharged himself from the ward, suspicion fuelling his anxiety. He was not well and had to return to hospital.

It may have been during this second spell when he had time to think, that he realised Jesus had found him. He persuaded the chaplain to give him a Bible. Each day he would go off to the chapel to read and think, and sit on the seat outside. Each day he would ring me for a chat. We visited him once. I guess he would have liked us to have come more often. He planned the day of his coming home to coincide with the Sunday meeting. The taxi dropped him off and he rolled in, pulling his suitcase behind him. He felt himself at home and among friends.

He cut the drinking completely and attended counselling. At Christmas he came and wrapped all the presents for Santa, but declined to be the 'Ho, Ho, Ho'! For our Christmas carol service, he brought the sandwiches again, cheese and tomato ketchup. The kids loved them. We invited him to spend Christmas day with us, but he was clear. He would be alone. He had it sorted. We had planned a New Year's Eve meal for our Sunday group, and Brian was all set to come. He did not turn up, and did not answer his phone. We were reluctant to pursue and chase him. That had never been our way with Brian.

The phone kept ringing, but it did not answer. Messages and texts but no reply. His wife had a key, and went looking for him. He had lain in bed a few days probably feeling ill. In fact, believe it or not, he had lain in bed, dressed in his Santa hat and Santa shirt he had bought himself for Christmas. He possibly knew little of the heart attack that smote him. He had lain in bed and died alone. Except I wonder if Jesus had found him first.

Footnotes

[1] Young Woman who lived in a Shoe by Elizabeth Braund p111-2, 2014 edition. Available on Amazon or directly from Providence House

[2] Extracts from The Young Woman who lived in a Shoe.

[3] From Except the Lord report p 26 in Providence House Archive.

[4] Young Woman who lived in a Shoe by Elizabeth Braund p159, 2014 edition.

Chapter 6:

Up the Junction:

Up the Junction

You walk out of Providence House and turn right into the pedestrian passage, where you used to pass the grocers and green grocers, Ladbrokes and the launderette, and now the Red Cross shop, with people sifting through clothes on the display rail, and the Zero Waste Hub, where Hadas and her team may be noisily food sharing with passers-by. Past the remaining brick steps, that used to lead onto Livingstone Estate, but now lead nowhere except to a bench for a smoke and a view of the world passing by to or from the station. Cross Bramlands Close, past the old chip shop, but now a council employment office, the sushi shop and the off licence, outside of which at different times of the day people are drinking or smoking – nothing much has changed there over the years. The Nazarene Church, with 'Jesus said: I am the way, the truth and the life', carved forever in rendered concrete. Then the station - Clapham Junction.

The other way to the Junction is right, out of Providence House, past the bus stop, past the bar, that for more years than I can remember used to be the Meyrick Arms, under the long and gloomy railway bridge, where young Abraham was knocked down as he followed his older friends darting across the road, but lived to tell the tale. Out from under the bridge on the left is where Dawson's builder's yard used to be on one side of the lane and the Job Centre on the other; but now Lidl, Boots and ASDA draw their multitudes to shop, and a Travel Lodge with café underneath cater for a more leisurely side of life. The Falcon pub is still on the corner of the junction, but Arding and Hobbs is no longer, although its historic sign remains as a reminder of the past. Left is Lavender Hill, where there was a Wimpy bar on the right, Dub Vendor for your reggae discs on the left. Straight ahead the main shopping street, St John's Road, where Woolworths once attracted the children, and even further the old Northcote market, long since gentrified. Right is St John's Hill with the modern station entrance, and opposite, where the Ruby cinema once was.

That is the Junction. Nell Dunn famously wrote her book 'Up the Junction' about Battersea people and stories in the sixties. Elizabeth Braund used to say she knew some of the people being described. Perhaps they used to come to the old Providence House. In this chapter are some of my stories, mainly written in the twenty first century, and written from my perspective as a youth and community worker. The Junction has changed, the demographics are different, but in many ways, people are the same. This is something of my Junction and its people. Up the Junction.

Two Hats

The key to youth work is relationships. Good relationships nurture growth. Good, trusted relationships can enable windows to open on a young person's life; but sometimes it isn't that straightforward.

The youth club was fairly busy, the sports hall bursting with energy. The newly recovered pool table drawing in the challengers. Outside groups of young people lingered long on a shirt sleeve night. Two lads showed off their newly acquired motorized scooters, when their arms were not aching with the problems of pull starting the engine.

He wore two baseball hats last time he came in, but today he was wearing only one. He picked up a boy's mini basketball and idly bounced it. He idly picked up a pair of scissors left on the canteen table, and idly cut the ball in pieces in the shape of a hat. There was no malevolence, just no thought for the consequence. While I remonstrated on the latter, he idly marked the door with the sharp edge of a pen, before I cut him short. Later he picked up another pen, was about to inscribe some rubric on a wall, but thought better of it. More than one seasoned helper had words with him.

The club had closed, young people wandered off, helpers gone home. I am in the office tidying up, when there is an echoing crash of glass. Two young people, apparently 'ramping' have gone through the window of a nearby shop. I rush out, and whoever was there, scatters. I phone the police and the owner and keep an eye on the property. The baseball cap returns, although innocent of the incident, but because he has seen an opportunity. He walks to the broken window, saying let's rob the shop. I stop him and receive verbal insults. Someone who might have grown up straight has found themselves on a crooked course, and either cannot or will not change. Some advise us not to work with him. The apostle Paul says 'hold out the word of life.' There are no illusions about the difficulties.

The spring suddenly feels cold.

Shining like stars

We have been living in age in which at the same time young people, searching for identity, want to hide themselves, cover their heads in a hoodie or a mask, while wanting their every move recorded on some instant media. A core part of being a youth worker is to encourage value in young people and what they do.

'Shining like stars in the universe' wrote the apostle Paul. There was not much need to consider the stars, while this spring afternoon was acting out an early summer. The temperature must have exceeded 27° by the afternoon. It was the perfect setting for a cup final. The team I managed were intent on shining like stars, hoping to steal some of the glory of the midday sun. They were serious and committed, but never self-doubting, as they faced longstanding rivals, with whom they had previously contested several fierce matches.

Amid strong challenges, first aid from the trainers, and sapping heat, the team fell a goal behind. An equalizer from a well-placed header brought the scores level at half-time. In the second half, Providence House appeared to take control. A powerfully driven shot gave us the lead, followed by a ball deflected past their goalkeeper. A goal against, a penalty scored by our team, and then a penalty conceded, but saved, and the dying minutes were frantic drama. Then victory and the boys felt like stars in their own universe.

A minibus of sixteen-year-old youths is a lively affair, before and after the match. Before the game a player on the fringe of the team, but with a behaviour record at school and the wider world that lengthened with his years, blundered into an argument with officials, and threatened them. I had to escort him out of the ground, from where, perched on a wall, he watched from a distance the exploits of his mates.

After the game, full of noise and chatter in the minibus, the boys asked if they could be dropped off at Clapham Junction, so they could swagger their way through the town centre, boasting to whoever would hear them. From then on, they began to ask, because of all they were achieving, whether they had become a legend in Providence House. In a way they had. I went home with quieter thoughts, replete with the emotion of their victory, sapped with the tiredness of a long day, soberly reflecting on working with young people, and how we can 'hold out life' to them.

The Night Call

Open all hours was not just the heading to a comedy show, it was at times a good label for a community worker. It was often unclear where the lines stood at both the beginning and ending of a day. Open all hours was never an advertised thing, but 'here for all' now embedded in our logo was.

It is 10.15 at night. The club is empty now. The building is dark, save for the light in my small office. I sit at my desk, reflecting on the day. A familiar face appears at the window. He is anxious to talk. There are tears in his eyes, probably he has been drinking. A look of bewilderment strains his face, and he asks why does it happen to me? But no, he does not want me to answer the question. Out stumble various occasions of personal grief: the bitterness of his parents' separation, the failure of his several relationships, his recent experiences inside, and most of the all, the child he is not allowed to see. Clenched fist, tear-stained face, and now head between his hands, he wants to pray and mumbles words – a belief that God knows and supports, and then a worry that perhaps He keeps him at arm's length.

He sees a Bible on a shelf. Find something that tells of a man being got at unfairly. I turn the pages of the Psalms and come to Psalm 17, but he struggles to read it. I read it aloud. It is apposite to his life. It is apposite to mine. 'They have tracked me down, they now surround me, with eyes alert, to throw me to the ground.' 'I call on you, O God, for you will answer me; give ear to me and hear my prayer.'

But where do we go from here? It is not a time for talking, but for listening. We have heard it before. It is never in the clear light of reason, only the uncertain mist and wind of his emotion. To recall his skill as a tradesman, even the kind work he has done in the club, seems not to help at this moment. He knows it is late, and that I should be at home.

It is 10.45 at night. He ought not to be here. An electronic tab is strapped to his ankle. His nightly curfew has long passed. Perhaps it is not the first time he has missed it. He insists that he has made up his mind: tomorrow he will go to the police station, and ask to return to prison to complete his sentence. Maybe a regular regime can undo the past weeks. He leaves, into the cold night.

A week later, and I have several times called his phone. Only the recorded message replies. I send a text again. I hear nothing, but I did promise to pray. 'If only you had paid attention to my commands, your peace would have been like a river, your righteousness like the waves of the sea.' Isaiah 48.

But there is something about being here, about being here for people.

'Mercy and Truth!'

I think in youth and community work there is always an element of serendipity. In Christian mission we better call it providence. There have been too many providences over the years to be a coincidence. Sometimes being there is a good place to be.

'Mercy and Truth!' That's what he always said whenever we saw him.

When we first met him, it was at Battersea Park. Providence House used to play some cricket in those days, and with our young West Indian ringers tried to wreak havoc among various church teams – with mixed success, according to who turned up.

On this occasion, it was a Friday evening and a group of us, some local men and some young people from the youth club, were having a net practice. A ball was driven from the bat of some budding batter, and strayed away from the area. A passing stranger picked it up, sauntered along, and asked if he could join in. The next thing, he was asked to play for us, and to play for the rest of the summer. I don't think I've ever met a man so full of cricket, almost all his maxims and advices were garnished with a cricket metaphor.

He kept in touch for the best part of two summers, and regularly enjoyed an early morning net, with myself and a couple of friends, and once attended a church service. He was always going to come to a Bible group meeting, but never quite made it! He drifted away from us, as he could never seem to organize himself; our cricket ceased and we lost contact.

Then he reappeared one summer, came to number of Sunday meetings at Providence and popped into the occasional junior indoor cricket session. Thereon he hardly missed a Sunday, and began to regularly help with games at our junior club. Bit by bit he opened the curtain of his life to reveal a Christian past in Jamaica, and involvement in evangelical churches, and baptism, but also of going off course, and keeping away from Christian things. For many months he would turn up on a Sunday, and have a kind word for everyone. He would stop the meeting to ask questions, he would scribble a note, so he could look something up in his Bible at home, he would pray in public if given the chance, and he would tell his neighbours to come along.

Then he disappeared again, and no-one has seen him since. Mercy and Truth! How providential even a stray cricket ball can be!

The Back Flip

It is a truism in youth work that we have more influence on a young person's life than we imagine, and in later years someone returns to credit the work. It is also a truism in youth work we have less influence on a young person's life than we imagine, and later on witness what we thought was influence eking away. Sometimes, of course, there can be redemption even in that.

He stood on the grassy bluff above the river Dart, and with his toes carefully feeling the edge, peered fifteen feet down to the dark waters of the river below. And then a spring, a whirl of movement, straightening out, and splash into the cold, deep water, and up again to the sound of cheers from the safer side of the river. A back flip well executed, and to please our little crowd, he climbed the high bank for a repeat showing.

We thought he had a lot going for him as a young teenager, growing up fast among the high-rise flats of his neighbourhood. Enthusiastic, quick to grasp new things, gifted at sport, performing in a well-known hip hop dance group, even awarded pupil of the year at age thirteen. He'd been away several times to the farm, and was one of the best, once playing the bongos at the harvest festival.

And then he did a different kind of back flip, that made a different kind of splash. Perhaps he thought it would bring some applause. Expelled from school by fifteen and into the referral unit process, and drifting more quickly than we realised with the wrong currents. Now arrested in possession of a class A drug, with alleged intent to sell. Now found guilty and arrested and sentenced to 8 months at a youth custody centre. Now away for a longer time for a more serious life affecting offence.

And we think that we have an influence on young people, and that for the short time each week that they are with us, we think we know them. And there are others. The girls that make the wrong choices they quickly regret, the young men following into something that seems the 'normal' course of action, not realising it can lead to shipwreck, and, of course, those who stumble and start at first, but pick up and find their way, and don't look back.

The Empty House

There is the life that the other half lives, although at times we may have to scratch around to see it. There is a difference on which side of the tracks you live. That was often true in Clapham Junction. To some extent it is still true today. There is no doubt that where you lives makes a difference, although it doesn't have to be an excuse.

Only the black cat lived there. That is, since the summer, when the family moved out.

They lived on the ground floor, on an estate near to Providence House, mother, two daughters under 12 years old, and baby, and the black cat. The middle daughter was fairly regular at Sunday school, and even spent a week on the farm with a club group that summer. Mother we got to know a bit, and Susan, my wife, would occasionally go round, and lend a listening ear, and prayed with her once. It appeared that in her distant past there may have been some, now forgotten, Christian teaching.

But mum was a troubled woman. Troubled by forays into drink, and maybe other things, troubled lest the children would be taken from her, again. She had met the baby's father in rehab, and so the cycle of difficulty had been repeated. Troubled by living on the estate, the pellet from a pellet gun fired, possibly at random by some bored youth, hit the baby, and they moved out.

Living with grandmother was not the end of their troubles though, as four more people to live in a two-bedroom flat, when there were already three residents, is not without difficulty. Susan visited mum in the old, empty flat, where only the black cat lived, fed daily by the neighbour's children. While they talked, the back door opened, and a lady and her two children walked through the flat taking a short cut to the corner shop. I wondered who else felt free to wander in and out of that young family's home.

The flat, though was soon empty, even the black cat had gone. He came to live with us, at mum's request. Sleek black coat, alert, nervous green eyes and athletic spring, he hid in dark corners of the house, behind the sofa, coming out from behind the curtain to judge if the way was safe, and deep in the darkness of the under stairs cupboard. He even spent a night above the false ceiling of the kitchen tiles; a fugitive cat, perhaps with dark memories of life in the empty flat, a silent witness to troubled human lives.

Sunday after Sunday we walked through that estate, collecting children for Sunday school, praying that for the time we had them, we could have an influence for good, or rather that the gospel could impact their lives.

The wedding.

Being a youth and community worker was never a job. Or it was never only a job. For those it was only a job, it was then ever only half a job. It was in reality a calling. There was always a connectedness to the job. For every youth and community worker worth their salt, it was always something more. That something more was part of the added value to being part of something vibrant, integrated, communal.

It was Redman's wedding. I got to the church on West Hill, near to Tibbett's roundabout, as my invitation indicated, at 1.30pm; but only the usher and three photographers were there in the empty, high-ceilinged church. One of the photographers was Brooks, who always appeared at photographable community events, and also dealt a mean, medium pace right arm over the wicket. Slowly, very slowly, the church began to fill, mainly at first with women; and barely a white person in view. I recognized several men, including Sabu and Manny. Redman eventually arrived with Caesar the plumber as his best men. The organist went through his repertoire, twice, got up to find out what was happening, returned to play some more, repeating the cycle until around 3.40 when the service started.

A guard of honour preceded the bride, half a dozen men, in coat and tails, on their arms, a lady in waiting, dressed in gold, the men turning into the right-hand pews, the ladies into the left.

Among the guard of honour, all 'Junction men' of old, with CB acting as father to the bride. We sang good hymns, the words of the marriage service were lovely, the couple kneeled for a blessing.

Outside while crowds mingled and photographs were taken, I spoke with various Providence connected men and women. The couple were driven off in a horse drawn carriage all the way to York Gardens, Battersea. I wandered off on my own, and returned to Providence House; but wish I hadn't, because when I eventually arrived at the reception in the old Caius House, a nearby youth centre, the guests were already seated for food. At least there was still a place for me. Cabbage Man played the music, the ushers doubled as waiters and Wesley was master of ceremonies. I was asked to say a few words, and I told a couple of anecdotes about Redman, mumbled some joke about being a white man at a red man's wedding, and briefly used the three-cord illustration from the book of Ecclesiastes in the Bible. I trust it meant something. Certainly, the occasion meant something.

I bumped into all sorts of people connected to our Providence story, including dear Alan Walker, who sat at the table, eating the food, taking the atmosphere all in, probably understanding very little, and repeating his mantra, 'God know everything.' That much of course is true.

Rosemary

I don't think you can underestimate the value of good role modelling. I do think you can sham it, and make it about yourself. About a good worker is an authenticity. It is more than skin deep. When you scratch the surface, it is still there. It is like Brighton rock, through and through.

Rosemary Bird was at Providence House long before me. She wasn't there at the very beginning of the life of Providence. She came first, along with other willing volunteers from among other places Westminster Chapel, to prepare Evangelical Magazines for posting. It wasn't long before she was drawn into the work with young people in the mid-sixties, while studying as a physiotherapist, then working as one at Westminster Hospital, along the Horseferry Road. She was one of those people for whom faith was something you stuck at and that stuck to you. When the new Providence was opened in 1970, and there was far more demand for people's time, she took a part-time job in Battersea, at St John's Hospital. My earliest memories of Rosemary at Providence House are of her arriving from the hospital, grabbing a quick lunch and straight into whatever was happening in the club, and the day not ending until the last sweeping was swept up and the last set of lights turned off. When the project to the farm began in that first year of experiment in the autumn of 1975, it was goodbye to paid or salaried work for her for ever. Somehow it all worked out, until her fall in the winter of 2008, from which she never fully recovered, and finally passed away on Sunday 10th January 2010.

I never knew a woman so humble, so patient as Rosemary, who in her fitness worked all the hours God gave her, and in her weakness graced her room with a smile, a look with laughter in the eye. Even in her last wheelchair months, she spoke with a prescient movement of her eyebrows, an understated word that veiled a knowing.

At her funeral, Rev Edgar Daniel described her as "a Christian lady who had no enemies, a fine human being with a deep faith, whose life was dedicated to the care and service of others." Bob Read, one of the first members of the old Providence said, "Rose never seemed to lose her temper, even when we played tricks something rotten." Doug, who came to farm as boy, man and driver, said, "I always remember Rosemary's greeting when I came to the farm, in a sing song voice saying, Well, hello-o-o-o." Phil, who came with many workparties as a teenager growing up and now leads them as a carpenter, said, "My strongest memory was being on the farm during lambing, and one morning Rose woke me up at 3am, and asked if I would help her with some lambs that had been born in the field. I quickly got up and met her outside. It was a very cold and frosty night. We found the sheep with two lambs and Rose picked up the lambs; then looked at me and said, "you bring the sheep". My hands were freezing, and the sheep's fleece seemed to be covered in frost. I buried my hands in the wool, and they were so cold I thought they would drop off. Somehow, I managed to keep hold of the sheep, and following Rose and the lambs, we got safely to the shed. That's when I learned what Rose's work was all about.'

It was said at her funeral, the shepherdess has gone home. Time and circumstances permitting, I will write a short book about Rosemary. She deserves it.

Everyone has their stories about people from up the Junction. These are a few of mine, and there are more to come.

Chapter 7:

A 303

It is one of those memories etched on my mind, the bigger shapes and picture clear, the details blurred with the passage of time. October 1975. Providence House car park. Not much has changed there - dark grey tarmac, in front of the dark brown brickwork, and white steel framed, Georgian wired glass windows. A white Ford Transit minibus, soon to be loaded with people, and a white panelled lorry, slowly being filled up with the furniture and paraphernalia, thought to be needed to start a new project. To a hill farm on Dartmoor. Me helping load everything in the vehicles. Me waving the group goodbye. That first minibus that went from here to the farm, and me not being on it; but little did I know how many trips in subsequent years I would make and how many thousands of miles I would drive up and down the roads to Devon.

Who was on that expedition in addition to Elizabeth Braund, the founder of the project, Rosemary Bird, her stalwart and faithful right hand, and Hywel Jones, who would pop up at critical times in the story both of the farm and Providence? None of whom are still with us. There is one photograph I can find and on it, beside the open door of the minibus are Derek Richardson, who stayed at the farm both boy and man, as helper and parent; Gillian Frost, who with her sister Zena, were the first on the list of so many early trips; Lloyd Richards, an intrepid youth always ready for any challenge, and who later repeatedly came to the rescue with mechanical problems of Providence vehicles; Dominic Palombo, whose life ended tragically far too young as a teenager, and I imagine his brother Eddie was there as well. But not me.

I had no idea. No-one had any idea that this project would work, and that the first year at Bag Park Manor, up the lane from Widecombe village, would be followed by the establishment of East Shallowford Farm, and that through every changing scene of life the work would still be going on decades later, even though the founding inspiration has passed on, with the work still thriving today in good hands. I cannot count the number of times I have done the plus 400-mile round trip to the farm. The roads have improved since then, as has the amount of traffic. Out of London, onto the M3 motorway, joining the A303 past Basingstoke, and following on through Hampshire, Wiltshire, glancing at Stonehenge eighty miles from London, through Somerset, edging bits of Dorset, until the road merges with the A30 in Devon on the slow haul of the Blackdown Hills; through Honiton and meeting the M5 southbound at Exeter, the A38 freeway and finally inching upwards onto the hill country of Dartmoor.

We will write more another time about Elizabeth and Rosemary and the early years of the project on the farm, but for now in summary. The first year was a rented property, in need of renovation, called Bag Park Manor, with a bit of land, in the shadow of Hambledon Hill, and with a small lake in which the Providence canoe could be paddled back and forth. It was, however, great for an adventure, or as the young people saw it, *their* adventure. For that first year, week after week pupils from Battersea County School, on Battersea Park Road, were ferried up and down from London for a ten-day different kind of educational experience, with the addition of Lettie the lamb and Trudy the Jersey cow, as the first livestock members of the project. Plus Hendrix the dog, a black curly haired terrier, aptly named, who Elizabeth had brought down from Providence House.

That year taught them so many things, not the least that the project needed to continue, and the next year, quite providentially, a farm came on the market, that they could purchase; and so, in the autumn of 1976 the story changed for ever. It was Pam who tipped them off about this property coming on the market. Pam was a local lady, who was drawn into the life of the work with young people. In the first instance she came in each day to help Elizabeth's elderly mother, Lady Braund, who had joined them from London, and lived with them at Bag Park, and then subsequently at East Shallowford. Pam became far more than that, and for many years was the cook for the groups who came to the farm, and served year in year, year out, winter, spring, summer, fall, finally hanging up her apron after Elizabeth's death in 2013.

They settled at East Shallowford Farm, in the West Webburn valley, a mile or so on the other side of the famous village of Widecombe in the Moor. At East Shallowford, they would go on to develop a small herd of south Devon cows, whiteface Dartmoor sheep, a workhorse and over the years several of her offspring, a handful of ponies, a pig or two, and of course chickens and geese wandering around each day.

For the first few years the Battersea school were the main beneficiaries of the farm experience, along with Providence House groups in the holidays. When the school relationship faded it was replaced for a number of years with social service referrals, and small cohorts of what was termed in the eighties, Intermediate Treatment groups, from Wandsworth Borough. The advent of Malcolm Hunter to the Providence team led to the development of working groups to build up the farm infrastructure and to develop the talents and challenge the aspirations of group after group of young people from Battersea and Wandsworth. Meanwhile from the outset, I learned the ropes of residential groups and minibus driving, until the point came when I seemed to visit East Shallowford with some group or other almost every month, some years personally going on that long haul twenty times. I have transitioned through a role on the farm as gopher to group leader, as key planner of the residential programme and confidante of

Elizabeth Braund, as founding trustee, when in 2004 Shallowford was registered at last as a charity, to chair of The Shallowford Trust. I cannot imagine a time, when age and health permitting, I won't be visiting the farm. To borrow a line from the Proclaimers, "I would roll 500 miles, and I would roll 500 more, just to be the man who rolls a thousand miles, to fall down at your door."

A Lung for the City

The question should be asked why on earth Elizabeth and Rosemary should effectively leave a vibrant youth set up in London, in the midst of a ferment of social change, and disappear into a remote valley and change their city dresses into farmer's garments, and become sheep and cattle farmers? Elizabeth's answer came in a phrase she coined: a lung for the city. Essentially, she saw London estates gasping for breath, as they began to bring up young families in concrete tower blocks on concrete housing neighbourhoods. It was more than a cry for fresh air and open spaces, or to borrow a modern expression, big green urban spaces. She analysed that something wasn't right, and she wanted to give a hand to putting some of it right for the young people and families she worked among.

She wasn't discounting modern home improvements, because she had worked closely for a decade among the deficient, bomb damaged, patched up community of old Battersea, that surrounded the Providence chapel, close to Clapham Junction station. She felt deeply that something had been left out, and to keep leaving it out would be harmful for the raising of inner-city children. She made social observations, but also theological ones. She understood her Bible to show that man and woman were designed to live in connection with the natural world that God had created, and to set their community in that context. If you take that away, then you will bring in a disconnect, and that disconnect may do some harm; for with it may come a dehumanising effect, a loss of belonging, a growth of the impersonal, a dilution of community. She wrote extensively about this, and discussed it with leaders of education, with professionals engaged in social work, with Christian leaders, and it led her to believe that her contribution, the contribution of Providence House, would be a place where this connection could be restored or developed. She wanted a farm for her people, where they could engage with nature, in all its raw and varied elements, work among animals and the land, to equip them with a wide range of skill and hands on learning, different from the more remote television education. She wanted some wild, open space location, where the horizons for a young person would be opened, literally, metaphorically, spiritually. She wanted it also because she felt that so much of the Bible message was framed in the natural world, that children growing up in the city would increasingly know less and less about.

That was something of her lung for the city, and to top it all she felt a God-given conviction that this was a purpose she had been called to, and so she must follow it. And follow it she did, and East Shallowford Farm became a lung for the city for countless hundreds of Battersea and urban young people, and families.

A few years ago, we asked some young people why they kept on coming to the farm. These were some of their answers. "The farm gives you the opportunity to be independent." "I love the tranquillity, beautiful scenery and the change from the norm. I also feel a special connection to Providence and East Shallowford." "Walking, star gazing, playing games, bedtime." "Without a doubt a place that reminds me of being at home."

A weekend to East Shallowford April 2013.

Every group is different, and affected by the dynamic make up of who is there, and carried along by the variety of the programme delivered, and maybe challenged by the strength of weather, which in itself can be a learning experience for the inner-city young people, and the bitter cold, or the seemingly endless rain, or in contrast those long light days of summer.

This group consisted of four boys in year 11 at secondary school, all soon to sit exams, with the intention of going onto college or sixth form; and also four boys in school years 7-9. The aims of the weekend were the same for all the boys, with the added purpose that the four older boys should develop some leadership responsibilities. Of the eight boys, only three had been to the farm before. Interestingly the parents of four of the group had themselves been when they were young people. The four younger boys were very regular attendees at Providence House Youth Club, and the older ones less so.

From the outset we planned the following for the group: to engage with practical tasks that gave both work experience and practical skills, and to engage with different people from the local community and across different generations; to undertake night walks to extend comfort zones and outdoor awareness, and to undertake a walk on the moors, learning to enjoy the countryside; to participate in a local community Easter service, and to join in discussion about values, plus to take part in a horse ride as a new challenge.

Day One. At last, sunshine and a begrudging start to spring. The journey down was trouble free and smooth. Dartmoor was clear skies and full of Easter travellers, hiking, cycling, rambling and dog walking - such a contrast to the thick mist of the previous weekend. We arrived at East Shallowford for a late lunch and to be introduced to our hosts. While the sun was out the group made the most of the afternoon, walking up to Corndon Tor, and back down along the river, experiencing at first hand a frozen bog, firm but bouncy until, over excited, heavy feet broke the ice and sunk into the squelchy mud. Over dinner the conversation among the older group drifted into talking about how much modern mobile technology impacts on communication among people. While washing up, one of the group commented on the value of talking among different generations. A night walk: it was a starry, starry night, and for many their first night out in the darkness. Perhaps tomorrow there will be less squeals and perhaps more confidence. It was a simple day, but already several of the above aims had been partially fulfilled.

Day Two. Spring has taken a step back today, with a smattering of snow and a cutting wind.

Undaunted the group set to the morning's task, stacking wood in the log shed, completing the moving of concrete blocks for a new cattle shed and digging a trench for sunken cables. An exploration of the marshy land near the river revealed plenty of tadpoles, but not a lot of other signs of new life. As an exercise in doing jobs responsibly and enjoying outdoor work, the morning was a success; but as a pilot for older boys acting as monitors for younger ones it was less successful, with the older lads not quite sticking to that task. However, the four older boys threw themselves into things, worked well under instruction, and showed themselves willing to take on new challenges - all good training. Lunch, chapel, and hearty singing to celebrate Easter Sunday. It was another good example of community engagement and inter-generational communication, as the assembled gathering spanned between 12 and 91 years of life. After the chapel, the cold wind had become stronger, so we kept indoors, the boys helping with preparation for the evening meal. The day finished with a night walk in the forest. No-one had torches, so we learned to adjust our eyes to the different shades of light. It was in part about confidence, and in part about listening to the sounds of the night.

Day Three. Horse riding. For most it was their first time. One of the younger members in the end dismounted, not quite having the confidence in himself or the horse. Even one or two of the older ones needed to be led by hand until they felt surer of themselves.

They returned full of talk and tales. One lad commented that it was the type of cold where there is no feeling left in fingers or toes. The log fire in the house put that right. Before we left the farm after lunch, Elizabeth Braund, our host, had a good talk around the fire with the older lads, about taking opportunities in life, of using their visits to the farm to learn from other people, from the countryside, and to develop transferrable skills that can be used to further their own life paths. Each had something positive to say about their few days on the farm. Two of the young people were fascinated by the birds they had seen, especially the hovering buzzards, and one wistfully said that he should perhaps take a year out before going to college to learn more.

Looking back. One lad spoke about teamwork, and that was true. The four worked well as a unit, and as a 'band of brothers', and in their way combined together to generally lead the younger boys well, or after a fashion. Another spoke about the value of talking across the generations, and they appeared to appreciate that. Another talked about having space, the physical space to do different things, the inner space with time to think. There was much talking, exploring personal questions and issues relevant to their age, among themselves, and with adults. In answer to the question, 'did you learn any new skills?' one replied, 'yes, more patience!' Most of all East Shallowford has given them the space and opportunity for learning coupled with enjoyment, for new experiences and ideas to develop.

London at 10pm was cold and dark and full of people. The four lads jumped onto a 345 bus and disappeared into the urban night.

The open spaces

One of the biggest contrasts is encountering wide open spaces. From the front door of a flat there may be only a shared corridor. There may be scrap of yard or a few yards of garden if on the ground floor. The green spaces are squashed between more buildings on the housing estate. The commons or the football pitch are more like an open space; but it is not the same. No way is it the same as the sense of space the young people – indeed of every generation – have experienced in coming to East Shallowford and Dartmoor. Even a single step outside of the farmhouse or of the new barn accommodation brings you face to face with the open valley, the hill rising to the sky across the river, and only the hint of a building or two half a mile away along the lane, that runs along the foot of the hillside.

From where we stood, we could see the river, grey, reflective, in the gorge below. It took the children a few looks to work it out, the river snaking its way through the woods, the trees beginning to thicken green from their winter bareness. We were on Bench Tor. It was 2022, and the group of young people were rightly hesitant to keep from the edge. Sufficient for them to appear to be on top of the world, the only sounds the wind. The wind through the trees, small oaks that managed to keep their foothold towards the top of the treeline, the wind through the rocks, the wind on the air, all different tones of sound. The thing that most impressed them were the crystals in the rock, the joy somewhat lessened when they learned their value was in their beauty and not in monetary terms, quartz and feldspar and mica schist.

A buzzard circled above in short then wider circles watching. A lone goose, long neck out like the nose of an aeroplane to guide its way, high in the sky, flight with purpose. A skylark or two burst from the ground, as is their wont, to distract our attention, and hovered and called above. The only trees that seem to enjoy these top lands are the hawthorn, wiry, tough barked, tenacious, facing all that Dartmoor winters can throw at them. Survivors.

Not much of this did the children appear to take notice of, but it was an introduction, and with time they will grow to understand and appreciate. Not so when we slipped down the steep slope to the beck below, sliding, bundling its stepped way to the river Dart in the gorge beneath. Squeals of delight in discovering this upland stream. Its waterfalls and natural weirs. Boots stuck in the mud as they squelched along the mossy, peat filled banks. Clambering over fallen trees, climbing over rock falls, carefully step-stoning across the stream. Sitting by a quiet pool underneath holly and birch. Finding their way up the grassy bank to where the minibus was found.

They may not remember for now the name of the petite violet on the bank, the name of the crystal in the rock, or why the lichen is so important, but because they loved the thrill of the hills they will come back to it, and that will be the beginning of learning. They will have remembered far more than we might give credit for, of their four days on the farm and on the moor. They will talk about it, want, we hope, to return, and who knows where their discovery will lead.

Into the whole kaleidoscope of learning come the images of sitting in the lounge with a Bible discussion, the dynamics of relations with each other, the daily routines on the farm, the patience of a long journey home with a minibus breakdown thrown in, meeting new people, seeing new things.

The Heart of the Matter.

The summer of 2023 will mark the end of my fifth decade of being a part of Providence House, and a proof that one year is not enough. It never was. There are many reasons I stayed so long, and one is because of the vision and realism of Elizabeth Braund, the founder of Providence House and East Shallowford. Beyond the mud and mayhem, anxiety and euphoria, there was always a bigger picture. I hope that the prospect of that has kept me coming back to the window. It is easy to miss the window for the desk, or the horizon for the immediate.

Elizabeth Braund was a hard woman to work with in some ways and many of the hardest times for me at Providence House have been in connection with her, as have some of the most inspirational, and the most stimulating to profound thinking.

My task at Providence House, and in connection to East Shallowford, has been to be a sustainer, a continuer, a connector, a facilitator. Hers was to break open new ideas, to expose false thinking, to press and dig below the surface of the value of what you are doing – why are you doing this? Is it enough? Hers was to challenge the confines of easy faith, to signpost always the direction to God, to Christ. Hers was the gift of storytelling, from which I learned and adapted to find my own voice.

When she ran the club in the sixties in the old Providence chapel it was a new way of doing things. When she expanded the youth work at the new Providence House in the early seventies it was a new way of bring community together. When she started East Shallowford in the late seventies it was a pioneering work. The Shallowford Nativity, the farm to the city, the city to the farm, were all her ways of making the connections to the story clearer and more imaginative. Her expressions the Lung for a City and the Heart of the Matter were deeply thoughtful and inspirational concepts that have tied together both Providence House and East Shallowford.

Elizabeth Braund in the later years of her life had a phrase to describe what this Shallowford was all about: The Heart of the Matter. The Heart of the Matter is all about connections. On this farm, you can find a connection with yourself, who am I, and find the space to connect. In that place, you can connect with other people, perhaps people you have never met with before, or from a different background – and that is community. There you can discover community. In that place, you can connect with nature and make all sorts of meaningful relationships with the natural world, and discoveries – and is part of who you are in this world, this great connected world of nature. But most importantly, in that place, you can make the most important connection, because I believe it is the connection that most fully brings all things together. To connect with God in Christ. That is the heart of the matter. It is the heart of the matter that brings us back.

A quotation from Phil Dorman. "I have been coming here since I was 14 years old. East Shallowford has played a big part in the life changing process of a troubled teenager to a successful working man with family and responsibility. My whole journey from my youth has been significantly impacted by the working together of Providence House and East Shallowford. What it gave me was an understanding of what a loving morally upright family looked like. It broadened my horizons to see there was more to the country than my small urban locality. As kids we never really had a family holiday, but East Shallowford provided that for me, and at times for my family, and has continued to do so with my own family. The stand out thing for me is this: in the city with so many mental pressures it feels like you are at times just existing. You are static. But away at the farm you are living. It is dynamic. I can also say that for me personally experiencing Dartmoor helped connect me to faith. Today I am part of the team of leaders who take groups to the farm."

Part of the benefit of coming to Shallowford, of bringing groups all this way, is the diverse richness of the experience, that means different things to different people. For those who came for a weekend and that was it. For those who came for a week and came again and again. For those who came for a month. For those who came for a summer. For those who came for a year. All with a different story. All with a different outcome. For some for whom it was 'once bitten, twice shy'. For some for whom they couldn't get enough. For some for whom it represented a season of their youth. Always it was this: staying on a farm, engaging with the day to day life of a farm, out in all weathers, living for however short a while in the particular space and climate that is Dartmoor.

Taking the cows out to the field and mucking out their pungent stables. Leading the ponies to their grazing. Following the pigs down the lane and through the gate into the space where they grubbed around. Feeding the chickens each morning, rounding them up each evening. For some assisting the farmer at lambing, droving the flock of sheep into the village to new pasture, supporting the blacksmith shoeing the shire horse, grabbing the sheep in turn for the shearer, hoisting the straw bales into the barn. Togged up and then below ground for a caving activity and coming out caked in warm soft mud, panting up the old railway track on a mountain bike, camping by a quiet stream away from the high road, stood on the tor to watch the total eclipse of the sun. Learning something about the past, exploring old hut circles, walking under the eery oaks of Wistman's wood, finding a long-abandoned farmhouse on the moor beyond Fernworthy Forest, and wandering round the ancient standing stones of Grey Wethers, and wondering why they were there and who put them there. In at the farmhouse, sitting in front of the open fire place, **broad enough to stand up in**, under the black ceiling beams, carpet over the flagstone floor, the grandfather clock from another century tick, tock, tick, tock.

Every sort of group for every sort of purpose over many years. For holidays and respite, for farming and work experience, for outdoor pursuits and nature discovery, for projects and plays and training. And family camping weekends. From 1986 until about 2008, almost without a break, we took at the high point five minibus loads of families from Providence, squashed them into every corner of the farmhouse or in old scout patrol tents in a field. It was a high point of the year for many, and certainly a true bringing together of Providence and Shallowford teams to work together in a good purpose.

Another rich seam of storyline with Providence House and East Shallowford travelling together is about families. Take Debbie Dowman. As a school girl she was part of the first years at the farm through her secondary school, Battersea County. Later as an adult she married Shane, who she met at her workplace Price's Candles on York Road. For a number of years, they lived in Milner Court, opposite Battersea Sport's Centre, where incidentally Phil Dorman and his family grew up. She began to engage with Providence House, probably as part of the cohort of people Malcolm from Providence House was engaging with on the adjoining estates, including Debbie's sister Tina, and mum Yvonne. Debbie's two children, Anita and Shane, started to attend Providence and then the farm. Anita now is a trustee of the Shallowford Trust, and Shane attends at least one working group a year to the farm. Debbie's husband Shane went on a number of visits to East Shallowford, before illness prevented further visits, and now grandson, also called Shane, visits with his family from time to time, and granddaughter Myalie is a regular youth visitor. Debbie is now regularly cooks at both Providence and Shallowford. To complete the circle, Debbie's dad, Tony, used to drive minibuses to the farm. There are more examples of family involvement over several generations. It is almost as if for many, once you have been down the A303, you have to keep returning

This old farm seems like a long, lost friend

It is a funny thing to say that I stayed at Providence, in part because of East Shallowford Farm, as it probably brought me more grief over the years than all the shenanigans of disruptive youth at Providence House. But what it gave me, as it has given to countless numbers of people, is an enriched life. A home from home, a belonging, a connection with nature and God's world to make your own, a spaciousness, a challenge, a place of both re-connection and a healing.

On a visit to the farm, I interviewed some of the eleven-year-old children about their experience, and young Jeremy said that he liked the farm because it was 'earthy!' I too like the farm because it is earthy. Sometimes I used to drive the minibus out of the farm gates, turn leftwards up the steep hill, and start to sing the words of a John Denver song: 'Sometimes this old farm feels like a long, lost friend. Yes, 'n, hey it's good to be back home again.'

It is a long way from Wandsworth to Widecombe. Almost each time I drive, I think or someone says, it is a long way to ferry children for a week or a weekend. Couldn't there be somewhere nearer. The answer is no, and each time it is no for at least something like this reason. When having laboured over hill and dale, along long grey roads for what seems an age, and having chugged up onto the moor, from Bovey Tracy, the last lowland town, past Haytor and its almost symbolic rocks, you turn the brow of Widecombe Hill, and you see it for the first time properly. The great sweep of Dartmoor, and its green hills rolling backwards seemingly forever. You know it's not for ever, and you know it is not a mountain top, but you know it is nothing like London, and all of a sudden, your eyes are opened to something bigger, something broader, and we are going there, into its heart, through its doorway.

East Shallowford is an 83 acre hill farm, of which about 38 acres are for grazing, 15 acres by the river is wetland, with mixed woodland and what they call rhos pasture, which is good conservation habitat, and a further 30 acres of rough moorland. People have been farming this land since the bronze age, as we uncovered the remains of a hut circle to prove it. It is mentioned in the Doomsday Book, and the farmhouse is an old Dartmoor longhouse, with fourteenth century foundations, and add-ons ever since. The courtyard square of farmyard buildings is a protected curtilage, which for planning and historical purposes we must protect. We have developed the old buildings into modern spaces with up to date accommodation, and meeting and activity rooms, and bit by bit replaced the animals' barns that had served their time in Elizabeth's day, with modern buildings better for the animals as well as for the engagement for young people.

To celebrate all this development, in 2022 we were pleased to have their royal highnesses, the Earl and Countess of Wessex to officially open the new development. At the opening ceremony we said that the new building work is like a gateway, that connects to the past and the vision that God put into the faith and energy of our founding leaders, and a bridge to future opportunity, many future opportunities.

Young people and families are still coming through that gateway, and the next generation of the East Shallowford team is acting as welcomers and educators. And this, we are still firing up the engine of the minibus outside Providence House. And this, we are still burning rubber on the A303. And this, we are still turning the brow of Widecombe hill to open up the vista of new opportunities. And that is the heart of the matter.

Chapter 8:

Goals

A murky autumn evening in west London in the early eighties. The blue Bedford minibus slowly driving past HMP Wormwood Scrubs. That should have been a sign of itself. Into what was called West London Stadium. Just to play in something called a stadium was a fair step up from parks football. The lads were proud to be in the cup final of the Association of Combined Youth Clubs competition. The ACYC was an amazing confederation of youth groups that for many years provided inter-club activities in London, under the genius leadership of Ernie Randall, until sometime after his retirement, it went down a cul de sac of thinking too strategically and distancing itself from the everyday interests of boys and girls.

Our opponents were St Matthews from Brixton, who for many years had led the way with football in this league. The age group was under fourteen, and our lads had steadily developed and grown in stature to the point where they should be challenging for cup finals and league titles. Only the mist came down. It came down so thick that you could not see one end of the pitch from another. It was never going to be a game of football, but would turn into a game of chance. It was hard to see how our players could use their wing play and their attacking from the back. It was hard to see how as team manager how I could impact play tactically or psychologically. It was hard to see. Full stop. Fortunately, the referee found it hard to see, and he abandoned the game during the first half, with Providence House one nil down.

The re-match was in sunshine. At Delta Limited's sports ground, somewhere down the A3. I had every confidence that our sun would shine on that day. So confident in fact that I handed over the coaching of the side to Terry Houston, while I spent the afternoon taking photographs. We won five goals to one. That team was, I think, the first time I had come to understand something about what a team could and should look like. David Graham quick of eye and sure of touch at the back, Tayo Olowe all energy in the midfield, Chris Crawley adaptable to almost any position on the pitch, along with a group of local lads who could play together, thrive together, succeed together. Terry took over the running of this team, with great aplomb, achieving success in Croydon leagues as well as closer to home. Our sense of greatness was somewhat put into perspective, when we faced an academy team in a south London cup final, and learned that were more levels to climb.

Football was a part of the Providence House story almost from the beginning. When I arrived in 1973, there were five age groups, all of whom appeared to be run by Rosemary, although I don't quite know how. When I carried on after Rosemary left for the farm project on Dartmoor, we seemed to be running seven teams, and again I don't quite know how. For a while Doctor Who drove the minibus, until I learned to drive. His name was Nigel Mason, but he wore a scarf like the Doctor of the day. None of us were trained coaches. Some of us barely seemed to know one end of a ball from another. Too often fielding a team was a scramble round young people's houses to make up numbers. Too often we had gathered a competent side, only for it to be weakened because Johnny was at his dad's or Billy was still out shopping with Mum, or whatever.

However, there was so much natural talent around that our teams were always competitive. Whenever since those half-forgotten days, I have met up with someone who played for Providence in the seventies and eighties, they all seemed to recall that their team was the best, that they were a force to be reckoned with, that they all had one or two star players; and how wonderful is nostalgia and hindsight. What is true is that all those autumn, winter, spring Saturdays were of personal value, social value and probably of identity value. Without a doubt a part of their lives. For some it gave leadership training. For all it gave pride.

We were never a football club as such. We were a youth club, who played football. For many years we were the only youth club in Wandsworth who organised football teams. It wasn't until years later that as our football developed, so did the coaching side of the work grow. The football was part of what we did, and often the doorway into other things we did. As time went on those whom Providence House benefitted most were those who played football, came to the youth club, participated in holiday clubs, went to the farm, engaged with life signposting discussions and groups. In fact, for whom Providence House was an all-round life enhancing experience.

Football was mainly, but not exclusively boys. There were always one or two girls who would play football with the lads, but they were different days. When we did have some girls easily able to get into a boys' team, FA rules would not permit it. A young Fara Williams trained along with her brother at one point, but we couldn't sign her up. She went on to girls' football, becoming Battersea's most famous sportswoman, being capped many times for England's women. We did have a girls' five a side team, that won several local competitions in the eighties.

Winning and losing didn't always come easy. We had a football manager who thought that the way his team had lost the match needed sorting out with the wheel brace from the boot of his car, swinging in his hand. He soon found other ways to lead apart from football. We had a set of boys who found it hard to be a team and didn't always take well to losing either, and whose reputation was somewhat tarnished when they stoned the minibus windows of their victorious opponents, as its vehicle sped away along Este Road, Battersea. Not surprisingly they were banned from the league, and the club and some of the lads had to make reparations. Mind you another group of Providence boys were at the receiving end of disgruntled hosts. We had taken a small group of lads to a youth club in Streatham by invitation. There probably hadn't been the clearest of communication, and our lads were a little older than their lads, but there were also racial differences, and the evening ended somewhat precipitously, with our minibus been stoned while Hywel Jones drove away half of our group, while the others scarpered through different back alleys in Streatham to return under their own steam to home turf.

There wasn't really a home turf when it came to playing football matches in the first decades. King Georges Park for many years, when Wandsworth Council's Recreation Department organised the Saturday league, and later at Tooting Common, when the league having been through several iterations became the London County Saturday Youth Football League. On principle we were committed to Saturday football. Sunday was the Lord's Day for us, which would give young people the option of attending a place of worship, or following the god of sport. You can imagine where the choices were often made.

In later years, we established a relationship with Trinity Fields sports ground, so that our more senior teams got to play on an excellent surface, and more locally with the George Shearing Centre, where we were able to mark out a junior pitch, which was only walking distance from the club.

I can remember, however, one football match in particular at Wandsworth Common, which was another regular venue. It must have been 1978. It was the decider for the under 16s division, and it was between Providence House A and Providence House B. If I have got this correctly, the A team had already won the cup final. This was the decider for the league. At the Common pitch near to Bellevue Road. Adjacent to a pond. No referee supplied by the league. No-one to referee it except for me. Somehow, I had to be neutral. Somehow the boys had to coach themselves, as I was usually coach for both or either of them. The added curiosity was that the A team were all white boys, except for Derek Richardson and Trevor Gayle, and had some highly gifted players, including Mark Bradley the keeper, and Mark Leggatt the captain and striker. The B team were all black, led by Noel McKoy, who went on to make a successful career as a singer. We had one football. Money was tight in those days. Of course, at one point the ball went into the pond. Who would go in and get it? Or did we abandon the match? Muggins of course. I probably took my boots off, and waded into the cold water to retrieve the ball. I doubt I received any thanks for doing it. Fortunately, the ball didn't go in there again. Fortunately, after a close game, the B team won. I say fortunately, because it meant honours were even. One team had won the cup. The other had won the league. They were all winners.

There were better times. Much better times. It would have been in the nineties. We were at an in-between period. We had one team on the go, that experienced mixed success, and the running of the team was shared between Floyd Patterson and me. Floyd holds the honour of being the longest serving youth worker I ever had alongside me. At that time also, the Metropolitan Police were still holding their annual five a side football tournaments. They were legendary. Beginning with a local competition in each metropolitan borough, followed by divisional and regional knock out rounds, culminating in a grand final for each age group, boys and girls, at the indoor arena at Wembley stadium. Several times we passed through the borough stage, but never beyond the regional one. As an exercise in PR, I think it was one of the best things the Met ever did.

Almost the last time the competition ran, and Providence had several age groups in the competition, I had noticed a young man from one of the local housing estates would bring a group of junior boys to compete. I knew his cousins, but didn't really know him. Taking a punt, I invited him to bring his group of boys, and mixing with ours, start to coach football on Saturdays at 'Banana Park', officially called Falcon Park. In terms of football, it was the best thing we had ever done, because from that small acorn of a beginning, blossomed and developed all the oak trees of Providence House football success, to the era at which our reputation carried across south London for football pedigree, and with the many young people who went on to pursue successful amateur or professional careers.

His name is Andrew Newell, who personally later took on another sport, lawn bowls, at which he represented Jamaica in the Commonwealth Games in Australia. Following Andrew, came a string of successful coaches, Wilson Frimpong, Mark Powell, Michael Maloney, and out of the youth set up, Seon and Leon Lee, Bernard Asante, Dennis Twumasi to name a few. It was story of endeavour before it became a story of excellence. That first winter with Andrew we gathered boys and girls and trained and enthused them. The second winter we entered the Under 10s division, and lost every game bar one. The third winter, we won the Under 11s division. The fourth winter, there were enough boys for two age groups. And so it grew. Bearing in mind our limited resources, lack of funding, how hard it was to even raise basic fees from families, and how our few volunteers were always stretched to capacity, without doubt we punched above our weight, and the trophy cabinet at Providence House is still bulging with trophies to recollect a happy period of youth success, and indeed youth led success.

At the end of each season, as football clubs do, we would invite the players and parents and the wider Providence family to an annual football presentation evening with a noisy but very good-natured two hundred or so attending. There would be medals for top goal scorer, player of the year, and sportsmanship. There would be photographs and banter, and at each event we would seek to have as special guest someone the boys could look up to in terms of sporting achievement, and sometimes they were household names; and, perhaps most importantly, men who themselves were playing football professionally as an example, and aspiration as well as inspiration to younger players. These were special evenings and marked something of the sense that Providence was more than a club, but a community. A community in which life long friendships were made. A community in which there was no great hierarchy, but a warm and competitive togetherness. A community in which young people were valued for who they were.

For a few years we were supported in our football coaching by Chelsea Football in the Community, with a succession of coaches, including the affable Daniel Gill, who also organised under the auspices of Chelsea FC a trip to Moscow, and the opportunity to play in Red Star's stadium, and just gain a sense of a bigger world out there. Providence boys also had the opportunity to play in a community game at Stamford Bridge.

More important perhaps than finding a career in sport is that for a large number of young men this football has been an important part of their lives. 2023 marks sixty years of Providence House as a youth charity, and in it is scheduled a football tournament to bring together as many people as possible who have been part of our football story. However, it is quite a lengthy list for a small club, for whom football was just a part of what we offered young people, of boys who have followed a career in professional sport; but I will mention just three as it illustrates the richness of the story, as well as reflects what is a realistic expectation.

Byron Harrison grew up on the Kambala Estate, a few hundred yards from Providence, and with his brother and cousin attended youth and holiday clubs for many years; and, of course, he played football, both for Providence House and other local teams. Byron was a quiet lad, not pushy, but dedicated with a disciplined skill to his performances. He began his football career with the Conference South team, Havant and Waterlooville, and progressed through a number of non-league clubs, until he landed at Stevenage, then AFC Wimbledon, then Cheltenham in the Football League, before continuing with a series of non-league clubs throughout England and Wales. At the time of writing, he has made over around 600 professional appearances, scoring close to 200 goals. To me he is a consummate professional, who has made a whole career out of the game, without having to be a hi-flying celebrity. Hats off to him, or rather what a good example to aspiring young people.

Michail Antonio arrived at Providence at 11 years old, living in Wandsworth town rather than Battersea, but drawn to the prospect of football. His football career is well documented, an international player, and with a distinguished career with West Ham United; but in truth he was just a lad from the 'endz', who adored his football, revelled in the trickiness and skills of small sided and cage football. A mischievous lad he came to Providence for football and football alone. In fact, he said in later years he hardly knew what the rest of building looked like, as the small first floor football court was where he made a bee line for each time he came. He was a singularly gifted player, but in truth among other equally gifted players, who we might have put our money on to succeed before him. He would train with us Thursday evenings, train with his 'proper' club, Tooting and Mitcham, Saturday mornings, nip on the bus to Tooting Common with two of his friends to join us Saturday lunchtimes for a match, and play for Tooting on Sundays. He continued this pattern through his teenage years, without a hint of what was to come. Following a prolific season with Tooting, at 17 years old he was picked up, signed as a professional, and then slowly at first his career developed until it shot forward when he joined West Ham United. Perseverance, dedication, joy at the task were characteristic of him boy and man.

Walter Figuiera stood out from when he was young, but family inability to access transport to train with Fulham quashed early ambitions, and he had to be content to flourish with us. Chelsea, however, took him on as a teenager, and he entered the academy system, thus ending his career with us, but not his friendship. Walter is a proper Providence boy. Living in Pennethorne House, in the York Road/Winstanley estates he understood inner city housing estate life. With his brother William, he attended junior clubs, youth clubs, holiday clubs, played football, and of course went to the farm on residentials. With Chelsea he toured and scored, and trained and played, but as is so often the case in this highly selective world, he was released at the age of eighteen. Hope, however, has always burned in Walter's heart, and his professional football has taken him to Greece, Portugal, Ireland, with over 200 league and cup appearances and still counting. Hope continues to strengthen his aspiration to play to the best of his ability, while remaining grounded with his young family, and staying true to his roots and his friendship.

My favourite sentence in the Bible that relates to sport puts the quest for glory somewhat in perspective: 'Physical training is of some value, but godliness has value for all things, holding promise for both the present life and the life to come.' 1 Timothy 4.8. That in a nutshell is why we spent so much time delivering football at Providence House, and why we were never just a football club. Physical training, playing football, pursuing sport, with all the associated values of commitment, endeavour, partnership and sheer joy are of immense value, and to quote the famous, world record breaking Olympic athlete of a bygone generation, Eric Liddell: 'I believe God made me for a purpose, but he also made me fast. And when I run, I feel His pleasure!' But of more value, far more value, is how you live your life, how your treat other people, how you gain a balanced perception of this short-fused life, let alone a short-fused career. To impart a sense that there is both a present life and a life to come is a greater gift, than that of preparing the pathway to goals and more goals.

A story to illustrate some of the above. It was a dismal Saturday morning one November. The rain was just beginning to fall as the wind blew across the football fields. Providence House under 14s team was playing in the Saturday football league. It was the second half, and we were steadily recovering from an uncertain start, only ten players and a goal down in the first five minutes, and now we were building on a 4-1 lead to our advantage. As you might imagine, I was focussed on the action pitch side, up and down the touchline with my linesman's flag, bellowing instructions across the pitch to players.

Not so young Arry. He had been climbing trees. Now he was bored from climbing trees, and was definitely bored watching his older brother playing football. Coming next to his mother, who stood hands in pockets, shivering in the morning cold, he blurted out, 'Robert, how do you know so much about God?' Taken aback, I scrambled a few sentences together for his benefit, and in the hearing of his mother. Then the conversation faded, as events on the pitch drew our attention away.

Despite his running around and healthy mischief at Providence House, young Arry did take something in. He certainly knew a good question to ask. It is always the question for us at Providence House, believing in something other than the game. How will such like Arry, or his brother running up and down the pitch get to know something about God? Is that what aside, from the football we sought to do, bit by bit? Through the Bible stories we told, through the discussions we had, and through this, as the apostle Paul said:

'devote yourselves to prayer, being watchful and thankful, and pray too that God may open a door for his message.' Colossians 4.2.

Providence House has always been about opening doors. Football was one of them, but we always hoped for some it would lead to more.

Chapter 9:

Sunday First

Sundays were never a day off. They were a day that was different. There were no football matches, although we might play football in the sports hall as an activity. Occasionally a successful team would play a cup final on a Sunday. The three times we had ambitious coaches who wanted to face the challenges of Sunday football, we encouraged them to operate under a different name, or even under a different organisation. For us at Providence, Sundays were the Lord's Day, or Sundays were special, or as we later came to think of them, Sundays were First. It was a pattern that Elizabeth Braund began, that I carried on, and that still in some fashion continued into the second decade of the twenty-first century. In some ways Sundays were the most satisfying of all days, because at times the engagement with people went to a deeper level. In some ways Sundays were about the hard grind, of keeping going. In some ways, they represent an 'if only' part of the work of Providence House. I would like to think that they were days of grace.

I cannot think they were other than that, when I remember children waiting in the squares down Maysoule Road, and the cry coming – the Providence van is here! I cannot think of it other than that, when I recall a group of teenagers, Bibles open, and surprised at how the scriptures didn't flinch from saying it how it is. I cannot think of it other than that, even when I recall the Lodges and Laslo and Andrew Dumsday giving us the run around at the open tea time session, we ran for a number of years on a Sunday afternoon. I cannot think they were other than that, when I remember Tony

Trolley, with all his simplicity, who would come week by week to join the Bible study group, and who knows what he understood! But he came for a place of warmth and a place of friendship, until he was unable to look after himself any longer in his flat on the Kambala Estate. Or Margaret, for whom in her latter years, Providence had become her haven, her life source, and who with little faith background at all, and with stories to fill up any available gossip column, attended without fail, where only sickness could prevent her.

The pattern that was established for me early on at Providence was church in the morning, lunch at the club, and get ready for Sunday School straight after. Although I had been brought up in church through my family, and as a young man had been drawn to faith myself, and committed to it, I found church difficult. I was encouraged to attend Westminster Chapel in Buckingham Gate and later Grove Chapel in Camberwell, because Providence House had strong links with them through Elizabeth Braund. I am afraid that it felt for me that I was coming from one world, that of largely unchurched housing estate people, to another world, and there didn't seem to be a connection. It wasn't that the gospel didn't make connections, but that the church didn't seem to be hitting the places, that needed to be scratched in my day to day life. When I attended a more local church, I didn't find it much different, although culturally it should have been. When ten years in to my work at Providence, Susan and I were married, and we joined the church, St Stephen's, along the road from where we lived in Balham, oftentimes there was that similar sense of disconnection. However, we raised our family there, and grew in connection there, and in 2023 are still there, although in a different building. Perhaps I am straining for the sort of phrase that was said of Jesus, that the common people heard him gladly.

Church life was always secondary for me to Providence life, and almost church was something we did, or I did, on the way to

Providence House. For many years, our kind friend, Ros Turk, who for a while became the administrator at Providence House, and who lived across the road from the church, would cook Sunday roast for us week after week, prior to our slipping out to get to Providence in time to set and prepare for the afternoon. It was a well digested act of service. The wise at this point might say that therein would always be the weakness of a Christian mission like Providence House, as it wasn't connected to a particular church. That probably affected the lifeline of support that could have been administered, but it certainly gave us the freedom to experiment in the different approaches we took. Nevertheless, over many years it was to the sense of mission from a number of churches that Providence House owed its succession of Sunday helpers, in particular Westminster Chapel, Ashford Congregational, Cole Abbey Presbyterian, and to some extent St Stephen's. In addition to these, the volunteers from Careforce, who lived and learned with us at Providence over a ten-year period, and some of whom have remained long term supporters of the work.

Sunday School began at 3 o'clock, and there would be the usual features that would characterise similar church groups. What characterised our operation was the versatility of the youth club building, and also that our children by and large arrived without any prior scripture knowledge from home. What we hoped characterised our methods was that we sought to faithfully share Bible stories and teaching and address them at the level and understanding of those kids. The other feature, already referred to, was that we always – almost always - had a minibus, which would appear all over Battersea collecting whichever children were on our books at the time. The story of our minibuses is a tale in itself. What a difference it made. What a tool for getting around, what a tool for being known. Whether it was red or blue or white – Providence is here! would echo around the walls of the flats.

It is sad to reflect that over the course of my working lifetime the numbers for our children's Sunday work dropped from consistent highs of seventy or more children in the nineteen seventies, through to the time in the eighties when I distinctly remember our dropping below fifty in attendance, until eventually with only Susan and I left to work it, we called it a day around 2015. That timeline matches the change in faith practice over that period, and the growth of Sunday leisure and different social habits, and at least over the last few years, I would hope, the strengthening of youth work in the neighbourhood churches. It also reflected with some regret that Sunday afternoons for Providence had become the last thing on our list, and the busy business of the week too often rendered it be the thing left to one side. It perhaps became the case as Ecclesiastes says, that wherever a tree falls, whether to the north or to the south, there it will lay.

However, what is true is that well-presented, dramatically told, delivered with clarity and conviction, and on a level where the children are at, the gospel and the stories of the Bible are relevant, meaningful, and as engaging for twenty-first century children, as they were for twentieth century children. Providence House after school clubs in recent years in a way replaced the Sunday School work, and there sixty children would be weekly captivated by a Bible story with meaning. But in the older days we had the adaptability to use different ways to engage. In Elizabeth's day she would write an annual pageant on a famous Christian theme for children to perform in. For a number of years, we took the Sunday School out into the estate in summer months, and with drama, guitar and activities gathered a group of children out of the flats. On many occasions we used the Providence House car park as a public open space to draw people in, on more than one occasion building the cave tomb of the Easter narrative, complete with the stone that rolled away, a cross on a hill, and the odd palm tree made out of tall carpet roll inners obtained from a local store. One year – it would have been 1984, when the adjoining estate was having refurbishment work - a tall ugly corrugated fence was erected, close to our building such that it looked as if we ourselves were closing down. Instead to show we were very much open, we obtained permission to paint a 20 foot by 10 foot mural of Moses and his people crossing the Red Sea. In more recent years around Christmas, we have erected rough stables and mangers, and with music and drama, and of course food, attempted to draw attention to the something more, that is so easily forgotten in the season, that too often loses its reason. We called it Christmas in the Street.

The thing we have returned to over and again has been these words from Psalm 78, where the Psalmist, fearful lest the message of the past be lost in the fog of the future, wrote: 'We will not hide them from their children; we will tell the next generation the praiseworthy deeds of the Lord, his power and the wonders he has done.' Psalm 78.4.

Not that the children always got the message. I can remember being with a group of boys in the front room of Providence, having told a Bible story, having engaged with questions and answers, having already sung various Christian songs in the plenary part of Sunday School, when Colin Haines had a question: did I believe in God? That was a great question, but did it show he hadn't understood a thing, or that I hadn't communicated a thing? That is always the question.

There was another instance, which must have been towards the end of our Sundays for children days, when I had a group of three lads with me, and I had struggled to put across whatever I was trying to do, and recorded in my diary, that the children hadn't understood some core concepts of sin and mercy and salvation. Well, why would they have, since they didn't appear in everyday vocabulary.

Sometimes however the conversations were dynamic. On one long journey home from the farm, with a teenage Simon Walters sitting in the front with me, almost the whole journey we never stopped talking and answering questions about faith and life. The farm experience, of course, was a great place for conversation, for questions, for putting a context on things, for just being away and expressing what is in your mind. The farm, too, was a place to fire the imagination for the Bible narrative. Here is one such episode from around the year 2000:

'The morning's task was to turn the farmyard into Bethlehem. The morning began with seeming chaos, vans slewed across the yard, equipment unloaded, and helpers criss-crossing with seemingly random direction. I guess that Bethlehem, too, had been a flurry of activity to prepare for its avalanche of visitors so long ago.

Slowly our Bethlehem took shape. Animals were moved to appropriate places. The sheep were sorted in the sheep race, to be later watched over by the shepherds abiding in the field. A tax office sign was nailed to the door of the pig's pen, but they seemed not to mind. The barn was labelled 'Cold Heart Inn', and lighting and spotlights were rigged up in every corner, and finally a great star, lit by fluorescent tubes was fixed to the roof of the barn.

We were not really ready to start at half-past six, but then I doubt if Bethlehem itself had been ready. The yard was now filled with people, huddled around the tarmac edges of the farmyard. Braziers burned in the middle, surrounded by well-trodden mud.

The upper door of the hay barn opened and a trumpeter signalled the beginning. A Roman soldier announced the decree of Augustus Caesar that all the world should be taxed; and in the midst of people still arriving for the event, came Joseph, leading Mary on Smokey, the old grey pony. Slowly along the driveway, lit by burning torches, they made their way into 'Bethlehem', past the tax office, and the grunt of pigs, nervously past the burning braziers, and into the crowd, which slowly, almost reluctantly, opened a way to let them through.

To the inn, and a pause for a carol to be sung. The innkeeper, Sidney Williams, with his stentorian headmaster's voice refused them entry, but escorted them to the stable. Smokey was tethered to the hay rack and was glad of an extra feed; Mary seated on a bale of straw, while Joseph fiddled around. In the adjacent stall a cow with its young calf. She bellowed at the noise and intrusion, more concerned about her own young than a story of human birth.

This was a real reminder of the grace of God. A throng of unmindful people. The bare muddy earth, the smell and sound of animals. "How deep the Father's love for us, how vast beyond all measure, that he should give his only Son to make of us a treasure."

The crowd trailed away from gawking at the stable, and slipped behind the house and the worksheds, and into the field at the back. There the sheep were waiting. The shepherd had drawn them down with an offer of food, and they were grazing along a line of sheep nuts. It was an appealing sight. The moon three quarters full, and yet the field half-misted, and dark beyond the glare of hand-held lamps. The shepherds were squatting, their grey blankets wrapped around them. A firework set off, and out of the gloom appeared a tall figure in white, Richard one of our Providence team disguised as an angel: "Do not be afraid, for behold, I bring you good tidings of great joy, which will be to all people."

There is something so appropriate in the message given to the shepherds, people for whom the Lord himself was the good shepherd. The sheep scattered, and the blanket-wrapped shepherds, a Providence boy or two among them, hurried also to see this thing that had come to pass. It was not easy to hurry for everyone. The very young and the elderly needed to pick their careful way over the rutted path, at the entrance to the field gate, slippery with the footprints of many, and on into the yard to find the stable, where Mary and Joseph, and by now a baby, and Smokey the grey pony grazed some more, while the cow and calf continued to hesitantly keep half an eye on all the commotion.

The stars were out for this Shallowford nativity. It wasn't always so. We have had a misty, rain-damp nativity. We have had an ice under snow event, when few would venture down those deep, dark Dartmoor valleys; but this evening Orion with his three starred belt bestrode the south eastern sky, and the great bear appeared to watch over the northern moors. And, of course, our own star, a fluorescent diamond made of wooden battens, and fixed to the roof of the barn, the highest we could manage.

Our wise men made a curious spectacle. First came the boys holding burning torches, followed by three pages carrying a gift, and a pair of ponies laden with sacks; three mounted horses, two of which were the huge-boned grey shires of East Shallowford, Bridie and Barny. There followed several moments of confusion as the crowd seemed unsure about making an opening for Mary and Joseph to appear out of the stable. Doubtless there was confusion in Bethlehem at the Magi's arrival. At last, they came, and their gifts of gold, frankincense and myrrh.

As we sang, O come all ye faithful, the rain began to fall, warm and gentle on our heads. It was only a play we were acting out, but it was real enough, and it lingered long in the memory. After hot dogs and hot drinks and cakes, the crowd slipped away into a Dartmoor darkness, to leave an empty farmyard; but we trusted that what happened was not forgotten, and this gospel repeat: "The hopes and fears of all our years are met in thee tonight."

The next day the young people helped clear up as best they could, put things back into place, and made our Christmas farewells to Elizabeth and Rosemary at East Shallowford. Dartmoor was a picture in the setting sun, its spotlight beaming across the moor, and turning green meadows into gold. Past Haytor and the lights of the valley below and in the distance the sea. On through the night, past Stonehenge, lit up for Christmas. The motorways its own trail of stars, blinking with traffic, and into London, across the grey Thames, and its busy streets.

Each of the young people lived on different estates, and one by one I dropped them off into their labyrinths of brick and stone, until only I was left in the minibus, to make my way home, and register with my family, my own house and lineage.' *[1]

Providence House never really had a serious intention of becoming a church, although I believe we continued to hold a licence as a place of worship, carried over from the early beginnings in Providence Chapel. When I arrived in the early seventies, Elizabeth Braund was conducting quite riveting Bible studies for the small team at Providence, with the occasional big event when the sports hall would be crowded out for a special service, or drama, and often a visiting speaker of repute would address the assembled crowd. In the early eighties we began again to meet for a Sunday evening Bible group, once all the young people had gone home, and there was a period when it grew, and we began to use the first-floor chapel space, that doubled as a stage, but in modern times has developed into a recording studio and music area. There used to be twenty or thirty people coming regularly, including some who have remained in regular contact to this day.

To repeat what we said above, we never really had a serious intention of becoming a church. Our first mission was to be a bridge between people, for whom perhaps church was not their thing, and the message of hope in Christ. Hopefully we were that, but as is so often the case, if a man or woman is drawn to hear the Christian message, but doesn't actually engage, or as they used to say 'close with Christ', then they will drift away; and that is what they did.

Who knows, however, what was sown, and what happens to the bread that is cast upon the waters!

In 1984 we had our first child. Shortly after we tried an experiment of a drop in coffee shop, to which more people dropped past, than dropped in; but out of which we began some relationships that have lasted a generation; one such being Michael Middleton, who for many years was Providence cleaner, but was always a Battersea character extraordinaire. The next move a year or so later, Susan began a mother and toddler group at Providence House, which ran until 1999. Supported by a string of dedicated women, of whom Jenny Burnett, nee Eveleigh, Gill Tarlton, and Karen Harney stand out, and run enterprisingly on a shoe string, this group provided weekly nurture to young mums and aspiring toddlers, from every corner of north Battersea, and long in advance of funded programmes such as Sure Start. It was built on solid principles of child play for the toddlers, touch and feel for babies, and warm, welcoming conversation for the mums. This group took place each Thursday at Providence.

Flowing naturally out of the weekly conversation, came questions and searching, and a women's Bible group sprung up on a Wednesday afternoon. Armed with eager questions, this group of women came largely fresh in their approach to the Bible as a new book to them, but with the dynamic possibility of answers and a signposting to Jesus, as a light and saviour for them. This group visited the farm on several occasions and was the successful forerunner to many years of women's groups to the farm.

Some of this group still come to Providence, their toddlers now adults themselves. Some moved on, and we lost contact with them. Some, now grandparents themselves, stop us in the street, or pop in to see what is going on. Back to a statement above: who knows, however, what was sown, and what happens to the bread that is cast upon the waters!

I have a habit of pressing the wrong item when accessing emails, and suddenly find that my emails are re-arranged in a different order. While writing this book, I did it again, this time in reverse date order, and found at the top of the inbox a note I had written to myself in 2014. It described the comments of a small group of women who were attending the Sunday Bible group, and had obviously asked why or how they first came to Providence House. It is both interesting and illustrative of so much this account is trying to convey.

'Margaret: It was about 17 years ago. The first week I came to the meeting was the week Bridget Matthews left her husband, and I had expected to meet her at Providence. By reputation, I had been warned about Providence - don't go there, you might get shot! But now and for a long time it has become another home to me.

Tina: My son Paul was about 4 years old when I first came. He is 30 now. I was introduced by Malcolm, who I had met on the estate. I found Providence to be very warm and friendly. It has meant a lot to me. It has been like a home to me. It is where I can be Tina, be myself, and have no need to pretend.

Wendy: I first came as a teenager with my friend Lorraine Salkeld. Providence was a welcoming and safe place. Over the years it has given me support, helped me when I was low, and taught about Jesus.

Annie: I first came 10 years ago. It was by chance. I was walking past in a hurry and a bit of a panic as I had lost my purse. A man gave me an invitation to the carol service. On my return from the police station, I went to the carol service, and have kept coming since. I sensed a place of community, of safety, of cohesion. Looking back, I have gained a greater understanding of Jesus and of the Bible.'

Some of those, who were a part of Sunday groups or midweek groups, did come to faith or were signposted to faith, and ended up somewhere else; which in many ways was our task. Some however came to faith, or came to renewed faith and remained with us. One such was Tina, whose faith against the odds, brightness of Christ when days seem dark, persistence of belief when those around her don't believe, continues to shine as a light in Providence Bible studies in 2023. Still in 2023 that small group meets without fail to talk and share and pray and open the Bible as God's word, searching and finding. These words of Jesus over latter years have become the principle of this group. They were said in almost his last prayer on the night he was betrayed. He was thinking about the disciples and his close followers, and he says, 'I pray for them. I am not praying for the (whole) world, but for those you have given me; for they are yours.' (John 17.9). I have reckoned there are those who God has put into our orbit at Providence House. Almost as if he has given them to us, and given them to us for a season, and in that season we welcome them, share something of their life; and who knows what will happen. How they will change. If they will change. If they will benefit. If they will be a blessing. Then maybe they will move on, but there was a purpose while they were there. Something of this is summed up in two of our Providence values: connecting to God and belonging in the community.

One such person was Doreen. This is a glimpse of her story.

'Every day she comes past pushing her shopping trolley. It is one of those square four wheeled versions that provide a support for her elderly frame. I expect she has done it for years, but I had never noticed her, pushing past with her half empty trolley to the café and back again. I only noticed her now because she has been introduced to us, and now I seem to see her all the time.

Every Sunday she attends our afternoon meeting. It is a small group, and she is comfortable with small groups. She parks herself on a sofa, keeping her shopping trolley close by, and drinks her tea with three sugars. She has a smile that is half bewilderment and half curiosity. She is small and quiet, but I think tough and resilient. She has come because her friend, Tina mentioned above, with her winsome ways and gospel-friendly invitations, has brought her, and now she comes on her own. I am not sure, however, if she has ever, or almost ever, opened a Bible, but she does so here. I am not sure either if she has ever opened a hymn book, but she does so here. She always leaves before the end, but then it does get dark early, and to date she has politely refused a car ride home.

Yesterday was Sunday First. She came early and sat in her usual corner on the sofa with her trolley close by. She was reluctant to come down the stairs to the service, explaining that she was supposed to be somewhere; but clearly hesitant that a larger group would be taking her outside her comfort zone. Nevertheless, we cajoled her downstairs, sat her with her friend, and the service began.

We opened with a song, and lit two candles. We talked about advent and Jesus being the light of the world; and then about birthdays, and sang heartily, 'Happy Birthday'.

For it was Doreen's 81st birthday, and that coy smile of hers broke across her ancient face.

And then she went out into the late afternoon, because she had 'somewhere to go'.

There are countless Doreens. Some are in the church. Many are outside. This one, late in life, had come into our orbit. The church and society are full of the argumentative and the opinionated, the brash and the busy, the well-loved and the well-known. And Jesus has his strategies to deal with them, to deal with us. Jesus also has his approach for the Doreens. This is Jesus at work with them:

"He will not quarrel or cry out; no-one will hear his loud voice in the streets. A bruised reed he will not break, and a smouldering wick he will not snuff out, till he leads justice to victory.' (Matthew 12.28-20).

We gave Doreen a candle. Please God Jesus had given her a candle.'

We only knew Doreen for a year or more. We discovered that in the loneliness of her old age and having been bereaved a few years earlier, she had let herself go downhill, and we had begun to notice that she always arrived with creepy crawlies on her. I persuaded her to let me visit her, and discovered that her home and everything in it was infested with bedbugs. When I say everything, I mean everything. We worked with a social worker, and a distant relative, got her moved into hospital care; and then attacked the house. Sadly, not many weeks later, Doreen passed away; but she had been given into our orbit for a while, and please God, we befriended her.

For us at Providence, Sundays were the Lord's Day, or Sundays were special, or as we later came to think of them, Sundays were First. Around 2008, we started a monthly meeting at Providence House. We called it Sunday First, because it was the first Sunday of every month, and because we were saying Sundays were of first importance. On the other Sundays in the month, we held our usual groups for children, and on about six weekends of the year we would be on the farm. We had a slogan for Sunday First: that it was always welcoming, always made you think, always for all ages, and always there were refreshments. All of which was true, and we believe still true. At times we have struggled with the all ages, but never with the refreshments. For a number of years, Margaret Beardall would faithfully make sandwiches for the group, and after her death, her sons continued the tradition until Covid curtailed our operation. Since then, refreshments have been spiced up by Waste not Want not Battersea.

Sunday First would welcome a range of numbers, from fifteen to fifty, very often in family groups. Very often those who attended felt that Providence was their church, their place of faith connection, their place of belonging. Very often those who attended had another church group somewhere, but felt a resonance with what we were doing. Sometimes someone who unexpectedly attended, was helped, or not helped, and moved on. There was singing, there was prayer, there was a craft or introductory activity, and there was food. There was a Bible message, at times delivered with dramatic effect. Always it was about people, and thus it has continued, even as moving forward there is an attempt to rebrand and make it more amenable to young people.

On that note, I conclude this chapter, that Sundays were always about people, and a door that was open, to see who would come in. I have been trawling the scraps of diary notes I made in the decade that straddled the millennium, and have reflected on the apparitions of people whose names peered from out its pages. Just one Sunday evening in January 2001 to give a little flavour.

'By 5.30pm Susan and I were ready to start the group, but only Alan and Flo were there. Alan, a man with special needs who loved to just come and be there and would always choose number 8 in the song book. Flo an elderly lady with a mysterious background, who lived in sheltered accommodation by Plough Road, but found we were a place she could walk to and drink tea at, and meet people. Then Easton arrived, with a neighbour. Easton had first got to know us playing cricket, and it was also playing cricket years later when we last saw him; but he loved his Bible, and he found the group to resonate with his faith past in Jamaica. His neighbour was Salma, who we saw that day and then never again. Arabic speaking, thoughtful, she engaged well with everybody who came, but how much she understood with her limited English and our south London accents, I do not know.

Just as we were about to start, a man entered the building. Shaved head, enormous earrings, and what looked like a bad eye infection, he walked straight into the small front room we were seated in, saw a Bible, picked it up, leafed through it, and then started to incant a jumble of religious and personal sentences for about five minutes. Not quite sure how to engage with him, we decided to sing a song, and which point he fell to his knees, dropped the Bible, and then just as abruptly, got up and left the building, and out into a Battersea winter's evening.

Follow that! We did by praying for him and singing Psalm 23, The Lord is my Shepherd. We carried on with our meeting, singing a couple of songs, a prayer, and opening the Bible at Matthew's gospel, I was about to have a go at explaining it to this group, when Tina came in with her sister Wendy and her sons, Paul and Antony, and Wendy with her young son Daniel and baby Kieran; so we had to do what we have always had to do, adjust the meeting to whoever came into the group; and in this case a small group ranging from 8 months to 80 years old. Wendy, meeting a person for the first time, proceeded to share with Salma her life story. Wendy, at the end of the evening needed a lift to Thornton Heath; but then that was what it was - all about people. People and connecting to Jesus.'

It was always about people.

*1 Extract from Christ is Come – Advent Journal by Robert Musgrave.

Chapter 10:

A Week Upside Down

Throughout my working life, I have found that things merge together, and it is hard to compartmentalise. Thus family life and activities with young people, Providence House and East Shallowford Farm, social thinking and social interaction, spiritual perception and political understanding all seem to merge together, or shift and shape as one kaleidoscope of life's rich colours. Perhaps it was a failure to compartmentalise my life and make proper separation, or perhaps it was a mark of commitment, and that was how it is and how it was going to be. Certainly, I believe that I have benefitted from such a varied, interwoven tapestry, and I hope my family has been made stronger thereby. You will have to ask them.

At some point, around a dozen years into my time at Providence I started to write, initially in fits and starts, reflections on what was around me. It migrated into a journal, but again in fits and starts. It progressed into mixing thoughts as I read my Bible, with observations as I went about my daily business. Out of that I published privately for myself a number of books, including Looking Backward, Going Forward; a thinking aloud with the Psalms; and Chasing after the Wind, 100 days with Ecclesiastes. In the last few years, I developed a Word for Today, a short spiritual reflection often accompanied by a narrative about what I encountered. Out of that I have published Words in a Lockdown Year, which is what it says on the label, and To be a Pilgrim, which related a ten days in the Holy Land.

In this chapter, I turn to my diary for August 2011. It illustrates the kaleidoscope of images, alluded to above, much of which is typical, but it ends with something that happened, that thank God was not every day, for me, for us, for everyone. I have left the verb tenses as they were in 2011. The story begins with a Providence summer holiday club outing to Brighton on the last Friday in July.

Brighton.
How can there be so many apartments and hotels in one place. Along one long stretch of road as I walk back from the van to the pier! The sea is thundering in and spitting, as it hits the shingle. The rain is spitting too.

The old pier stands like a Meccano sculpture in the sea, a sort of demon of the south, a fortress of iron in a green sea. In fact Brighton does have an angel, a green winged statue of a lady, holding up some branch in one hand, and a ball with a cross on it in the other, symbols I think of nursing, and a commemoration of Edward VIIth.

The seafront is an amazing place of people just doing their own thing. Keep fit, skating, running, boxing, folk playing boule, people just walking, people who look as if they are waiting for nightfall so they can sleep rough.

The ornate bandstand opposite the Brighton Hotel is empty save for a young man walking round and round making a phone call.

I pause and take pictures of the climate connections exhibition. It is raining harder now but that doesn't stop the beach volleyball or the BMX riders.

The pier. It is a curious thing, a highway of colour and noise and people, stretching into the sea, that sways to the rhythm of the music. The best light show tonight is in the sky, now the rain has stopped, or perhaps because the rain has stopped. There is a fire over the hills above Portslade, a pouring of gold that runs behind the hills to tomorrow; and beyond it the palest of blue evening skies.

As the sun fades to dusk the evening lights on the hills begin to sparkle, and the tall lighthouse stands tall and dark as the night nears.

A group of our lads slip past, unaware of me or the sunset as they rush from one set of amusements to another. There are nine boys, four girls, Richie and me. I have a wad of money in my pocket so I better gamble it away and join them! The Lanes. I have never been there at night before, and was not really aware that it was such a labyrinth of cafes and bars and shops. Sort of a West End by the sea. Not sure if the group are impressed; there is nothing for them, but to see other people eating and carrying on. One boy is missing. Apparently, he has bumped into someone he knows. Meanwhile we are on the beach getting as close to the water as possible without getting wet; someone will.

Monday 1st August 2011.

It is August again, the season of writing diaries, for probably repeating old sentiments, and maybe with some new stories. A grey brown fox lies in the neighbour's garden, still as a stone. He moves as I approach, fixing me with his sad and wary eyes. I don't really want foxes in our garden. One of the cats has not yet appeared, but no doubt will. I send him off.

Today, Susan, my wife, and Mark, our son, and Joy, our eldest, her husband, Tom, with eight others begin their new adventure; transported by me to Heathrow, and then on to Peru via Miami. Sporting red tee shirts, laden with luggage, under one of those it will stay-bright-like-this-forever English summer skies, the team decant from the minibus at Terminal 5, full of promise, to participate in a children's project on the edge of the Peruvian desert.

My own adventure consists of being on the road for most of the day. Phone calls and hurried arrangements at Providence, then off with Phil Dorman and Chris Broome, carpenters connected to Providence House. To Eastbourne via IKEA Croydon. Filled with tools and flat pack boxes of kitchen units there is barely a space to sit in the minibus, and the day has almost ended before we arrive above my father's museum to install the lads for half a week's work. Eastbourne is hot, and the sea calm and inviting, but there is only time to politely agree to visit the beach another day.

Fish & chips and a briefing for the remainder of the week are all there is time for, before I head back to London. I stop by Dad's house, and I am afraid he seems old and alone, which of course he is; but he is sufficiently animated to show me his little archaeological digs in his small garden, and his piles of sifted stones, and lumps of flint on which he is convinced that he can see shapes and faces. He is certain that he is onto something, the more so because of the Nero Roman coin that he has found, gnarled and scratched over many centuries, but unmistakably something ancient.

Homeward but too weary to appreciate the evening hills, and pink grey sunset.

A solitary plane passes over the house in Norbury lit up by the urban lights. It is the wrong direction to America or Peru, but a reminder that at that moment somewhere over the Gulf of Mexico, Sue and the crew are headed south towards Lima.

Tuesday 2nd August 2011.

Summer rain falling on the parched grass, the eager flowers, and the red tent hanging to dry that I should have brought in last night. The summer heat soon takes hold and raises the daytime temperature to 30° centigrade.

Today has been a day of meeting parents of girls we hope to take this weekend to the farm. We already have Holly, Chloe and Bernice, Providence regulars, booked, but we quickly need to add to the group. First, at midday, a girl from a Kossovan family, and friend of one of the above, comes with mum and younger sister. She seems keen, and not too phased by the Christian background of the project, but asks that we can provide Halal meat for meals; she stays for the whole afternoon. Georgina arrives later, with mum, and with Dad, Phillip, who I have known for over thirty years; he repeats the same joke, that she can only go if I promise to lose her! She is shy, but she knows us a bit, though not the other girls, so I have invited her to come tomorrow to mix in and get acquainted. I pray that she will.

Three other girls come with their mothers at 6pm, two of whom Providence knows, but I barely know, and one of whom clearly has 'attitude'. The last mum arrives as the others are leaving, her daughter a friend of Bernice's. Mum seems pleasant and attractive, but we have not met the daughter, so we take it a bit on trust. Let's hope that Rosie, our daughter, gets on well with them all at the weekend, as our key helper.

The daytime club followed a similar pattern to Monday with a handful of stalwarts, whom we took to Battersea Park for the summer scheme event. There the lads saw the boy we suspect of stealing a blackberry phone at Providence last week, and think we are closer to its recovery without accusing the boy himself; let's hope it's not wishful thinking induced by the hot sun.

The evening club was busy, with only one altercation. Home was welcome, and I imagined that in La Florida, the village in Peru, there would have been some kind of welcoming meeting at the little church.

Thursday 4th August

Wednesday and Thursday have flown past.

So far, I have established an orderly start to the day. Fall out of bed just after seven o'clock, carefully step down the stairs, greet and sort the cats, and sit in the basket chair with a cup of tea, and briefly read and think about the two Bible readings I am following. Get up, try and write this diary and plan the day with a bowl of cereal, before departing for Providence.

I have reached John chapter 17 in J.B. Phillip's translation: 'You have given Him authority over all men to give eternal life to all that you have given him'. I think about our lives in His hands, our coming to Him, our being brought to Him, of our staying with him, or as Phillips translates in a previous chapter, 'sharing his life'. I think too of those in His hands, but not yet apparently there, or on the way there, on the journey as they say.

I am part way through a sequence of very interesting and longish Psalms, which each have definite and separate themes, that I would like to write or talk about if occasion permitted. I have reached Psalm 107, where the refrain is 'Let them give thanks to the Lord for His unfailing love and his wonderful deeds for mankind', and where the song declares all sorts of situations where God has shown His grace through rescue, through nurture, through giving.

Well, I trust that His unfailing love has been evident in the last couple of days. Wednesday was into Providence to get ahead with planning etc in the morning, and being busy with the procession of young people throughout the day, never full but always people in, people to see, people to call or speak to.

Thursday, I stayed at home and used the conservatory as an office, leaving others to run the club, and by one o'clock I was on the road, via ILEA and B&Q again, and off to Eastbourne. It had rained all night and day, but by the afternoon, the sun was warm and the skies were bright, the Downs were ever inviting to enfold, the seagulls alluring in their seaside calls. Unfortunately, although Phil and Chris had done a great work, the kitchen was not finished and we will return next Saturday to complete.

Home after 11, with Rosie already tucked into bed.

Friday 5th August.

This is travelling day, the next of the sequence of farm groups. Rosie and I bid farewell to the cats, stocked them up with biscuits, drinks and a bowl full of meat and left before they could phone 'Catline'. To Joy's home to check her flat and feed the plants in the bath, but not properly thinking where I was, put the key into the first flat on the landing, only to be greeted from behind the locked door with, 'who's there'; with hurried apologies, I beat a retreat and entered Joy and Tom's Flat and gave it a brief glance of approval.

Thinking again of Jesus' words about all that the Father has given Him, I thought about our responsibility for this group of girls who have been given into our charge. In some ways it is a social responsibility as well as a spiritual responsibility.

Yesterday Georgina dropped out of the group, and today the mother of another phoned to say her daughter had cold feet, and was unsure about going. I spoke to her on the phone and it seemed to make no difference; Jamel, our assistant youth worker, later from Providence spoke to her, and it seemed to trigger the right response, so when everyone was present, we collected her in Tooting. Eight girls, then, Rosie and me; Chloe, Holly and her friend Lidra, Bernice and her friend, who it appears is the niece of one of my former football captains, another couple of girls, who through Jamel, our youth worker, have attended a few activities this summer, and the girl who no longer has cold feet.

It was a good ride westward, but for traffic flowing eastwards it was a real stop and go affair. By the time we reached Dartmoor, the journey had possibly begun to wear on some of the girls, but our arrival at Shallowford was timely. The cow was being milked and the pigs being fed, and Tim the dog was welcoming and exuberant as ever. Miss Braund was on good form and the introductions to the farm seemed to work well. Dinner was a pleasantly social affair, and the signs for the weekend are that it will be lively.

There is nothing like wild life to gain the interest of young people. On the road to Bellever we saw several very young calves on the road with their mothers and also young foals. There was a period of around four years when we couldn't stay overnight at the farm, and discovered Bellever Youth Hostel, as a welcome resource just three miles away. At the hostel, Garry, the hostel warden, let the girls see him rescue a bat that had wandered into the building. The only downside of the nature experience was the great number of very small flying insects hovering on a bedroom ceiling in one of the rooms. A quick room swap with Rosie and me, and all was well, and we nodded off hoping the flies would fly off elsewhere in the night.

Saturday 6th August 2011.

This was a good day. I think everything seemed to work well. On arrival at East Shallowford, the house was barely ready to receive visitors, so Rosie diverted the group with an exploration of the farm, and helped Paul Edworthy, the young man who manages the farm, with some basic routines; then the girls put on green fingers and got stuck into gardening. Without complaint they dug, and cut, pulled up bracken and nettles, and under supervision, put in a fair effort, to make an impression on the garden area.

Then off to Shaldon for the afternoon. Fish and chips on the beach, with half an eye watching events on the water, the Lifeboat association performing rescues, various stalls and activities on the strand and Captain Jack Sparrow wandering around. It was the Shaldon Water Carnival, and the afternoon climaxed with the dressed-up floats passing back and forth along the estuary.

Shaldon is an attractive little resort, its line of houses stretching along the southern side of the Teign estuary, whose waters begin on the high moor, with cottages backed up to the cliff behind; Teignmouth across the water with its tall boat repair workshops, and out beyond the harbour the open sea. The girls scrambled over the rocky boulders under the red sandstone headlands, and round into the open beach to swim and paddle, and return via the tunnel through the cliff.

During the quiet periods the girls seem able to get along, talk and play games quite amicably, and dinner times have so far been quite pleasant, thirteen of us sat around a square table with conversation flowing freely. This group is experimental in some ways, as not all the girls are well acquainted with Providence or each other, but they are growing together. There is no spiritual revolution here but we do hope that in the background a picture may be forming through the little nuances and patterns of work, the saying of grace, the delight in nature.

Sunday 7th August 2011.

Grey skies, blue skies, clouds on the move, dozens of swallows swooping, calling, feeding, all around the edge of the forest at Bellever. My day is beginning at 7 o'clock with a cup of tea; La Florida in Peru is yet to waken, but in a few hours' time, I will imagine Sue and crew walking to the end of the road, and hailing a lift to the village for the first full church service, and I pray that the Lord will indeed be present.

For our part, we are away and across the moor to Sticklepath. There is a community church here, that meets in the village hall, though this morning it was in the back kitchen area, as the main hall was being decorated. The church is run by farmers and builders and workers, very informal, very evangelical, full of strong Devon accents, and warm Christian speaking. It was an informal sharing service, where members and children were asked to bring an object, and say something about it as a parable. We asked our girls to make up a song, which they did over breakfast, and sang well, to a Bruno Mars tune, in the current pop charts. Although the service took over an hour, the group were so friendly chatting over tea and cake afterwards, that I reckon the overall impression was good.

Not far from the village is Belstone Tor, to which we drove and had a windy picnic before it rained on our parade. For most of the girls this was their first introduction to the moor, and the rain and shine of Dartmoor. Belstone Tor and its several high points were clambered over enthusiastically, and with our nine girls we went in search of the Nine Maidens, standing in a stone circle, apparently frozen in motion from dancing on the Sabbath. Apart from one of the girls twisting or spraining her ankle, and everybody getting soaked, it was an enjoyed experience.

Back at the ranch the girls dried out in front of the fire, helped in the kitchen, and watched the old film of the Pilgrim's Progress, made at the farm years ago, with Miss Braund giving a pretty lucid commentary. Sunday dinner was a lively meal, with the girls feeling sufficiently at home to chat and giggle, and be comfortable as a Shallowford family.

Last night.

Monday 8th August 2011.

This could not have been a more contrasting day, as we left Bellever Youth Hostel to the call of the swallows, and crossed the granite bridge of a softly flowing River Dart, making our way to East Shallowford for the last time; and at the end of the day arrived at

Clapham Junction, amid the sound of police sirens, rampant youths attacking shops, and worried people gingerly finding a way home.

At the farm, the last activity arranged for the girls was a walk with a local naturalist along the river to see what could be seen and to stimulate their curiosity. To their surprise they found a lizard warming in the sun, a large frog in the mud and disturbed a grass snake under a log, and identified a host of butterflies.

We left the farm after lunch, the girls having made a good impression on the farm, and the farm on the girls, all eager to be home, and eager to return again.

At around 5pm, having sent a text giving our eta, I received a message to warn me that, according to social media information, riots would begin at Clapham Junction around 8pm; a short while later a call from Providence advised me to avoid Clapham Junction as there was trouble. Taking a back way through Wandsworth, we arrived on Plough Road to see a group of youths marching furiously, and then attacking the shuttered store front of a local shop. There were girls among them, but no faces that I recognised. Apparently, this same group had gathered in Shillington Park where our guys were earlier conducting a football coaching session. Passing the back of Clapham Junction, we noticed the police cars, and sensed the uncertainty. Traffic was almost at a standstill as we turned the corner to Providence House.

Providence car park was full of spectators and club members – apparently the gang I had seen a few minutes earlier had congregated for a while near our building before moving on into the estate. Apparently, they did not attempt to enter, but our staff said they were ready if they had! A couple of the girls' parents said we should have stayed on the farm.

Eventually we closed the youth club, and I, the last to leave, got into the minibus to go home. Clapham Junction itself seemed very crowded, so I elected to take the slip road past Asda to Lavender Hill; the odd police car was strategically placed, while groups of people gathered, and many hooded and bandanna-ed young men moved along the road. There seemed little point in hanging around, and I was weary from a long journey. En route home I avoided London Road towards Thornton Heath, having heard on the news that there was trouble towards West Croydon. As we neared our house, I asked Rosie if the columns of black clouds were smoke or the threat of dark rain; later I learned that it was the pall of smoke from Reeves Corner, burning into the night. It was the furniture business at Reeves Corner, we had known as children, and apparently the Reeves family had started it in Victorian times; it was a landmark everyone knew.

While we ate and watched the continuous television news, we learned of the extent of the troubles in Croydon and also at Clapham Junction, with graphic pictures of looting in St John's Road and Lavender Hill. So Rosie and I went back to Providence, and sat for a few minutes in the car park. The building was secure. I watched some youths looking through their 'trophies' by the side of the road, and then one of them, dressed in red from tip to toe came over to me, and asked if I was police; 'no, I'm just making sure my youth club is safe'. Then he looked from behind his red bandanna with a sort of recognition: 'I used to come here as a kid, no-one will trouble this building'. His companion called my name and wandered off. Perhaps there is some twisted comfort there.

Across the road, the corner shop had been broken into, shutters forced open, and the shop now turned into a self-service store. Trusting the security of our building to God and to some youth villain's moral code, we drove slowly round the estate, and then up to Clapham Junction. By now the police seemed to have secured St John's Road, though I heard that later it came under renewed attack. Up Lavender Hill, various shops were smashed, including the Bible bookshop. Large crowds hovered, many just watching, tourists to a new curiosity. Others masked or with hidden faces roaming menacingly. Effectively the whole shopping precinct was smashed with large scale looting. Later on, the Party Shop was ablaze, allegedly through helium canisters being ignited.

Not needing to be a part of the spectacle, nor wishing to be caught up inadvertently in it, Rosie and I made our way back across south London. Balham and Streatham seemed unaffected, though I later heard the Cash and Carry shop was broken into. In Norbury, the amusement arcade was smashed up, and the computer store, and as we turned into our road, saw the police arresting a man outside Tesco's, which too had suffered damage.

The sounds of the night were not those of the wind in the trees, the cackle of the cockerel, the cry of a sheep in the breeze. This was indeed far away from the farm.

Tuesday 9th August

As soon as we were up, Rosie and I drove to Clapham Junction, and found to our relief that Providence House was secure. Only the corner shop had been looted, and a failed attempt at the store next to it, but the rest of our parade was untouched, the Red Cross shop, the cafes, the hairdressers, the undertakers and the motor bike spare parts shop. But Clapham Junction was sealed off, and policemen manned the barriers of tape cordons, and almost like a border crossing there was a continuous traffic of people coming to the boundary trying to have a look. I met one young man, who regretted he had not been there the night before, and had missed a once in a lifetime experience!

All morning the forensic teams conducted their meticulous inspections, and the great and the good put in an appearance, including London Mayor Boris, and Teresa May the Home Secretary. By the afternoon the broom brigade of volunteers came in and swept away the glass and debris but not the memories.

At Providence House, we are in the middle of a daytime holiday youth club, and a trickle of young people and visitors came in and out all day. We opened, too, for the evening junior club, but not a single person came, parents clearly reluctant to let their children out of their sight. The local shops also closed early and let down the shutters with renewed security. But in truth, like a storm that has moved on, there was little likelihood that the lust for looting would return for a second night of all night shopping.

This was a day of talking, and hearing eye witness accounts, but also imaginary tales, for example, how that MacDonald's was broken into and the rioters started to cook the chips! I was told of a lady who opened her suitcase on the floor and sent her children into the shop to fill it up with looted goods. Every age of person seems to have joined in the lust for goods. Several people who came to talk with me had been there as spectators, as the audience to a spectacle enacted before them, of theft, of aggression, of destruction, and until later in the evening of the police impotent to intervene, until the reinforcements came and armoured cars slowly entered the scene.

This was a day, too, of opinions, of every shade of thought, of every theory. All day long we kept the television on in Providence House, and heard the dismal picture of London's turmoil, growing gloomier by the hour, and then the fresh reports of trouble in Manchester and elsewhere in the evening.

There is a new kind of tourism, and I confess that I succumbed to it. I walked to the Junction late in the day, and joined the crowds wandering around, cameras in hand, as if surveying the ruins of a Roman city. Lavender Hill was cordoned off, but elsewhere we were free to walk among the myriad of glaziers and carpenters boarding up. In a weird way it was a peaceful and friendly scene, workmen efficiently going about their business, and the procession of the curious ambling along, pausing to take a photograph, chatting with strangers.

The first place you pass at the end of Falcon Road is the gym, and there a sign stands boldly: 'Fitness First – Our Goal? - Achieving Yours'. I was sure there was some irony there as I passed onto the high street, and saw shop after shop smashed. Hardly a store escaped along St John's Road. Waterstones was untouched – perhaps the looters don't read; so too was Ryman's – perhaps they don't write either. Up Lavender Hill, from the Junction to the last shop before the library, the 'eat all you can' Chinese Restaurant, every shop had a smashed window. None were spared in an orgy of destruction. There was one other exception: Dub Vendor the record shop. Perhaps that tells a tune. Most sombre of all, however, was the dark empty shell of the burnt-out party shop.

Leaving that scene, I took the minibus to drive home, but decided to go on further into Croydon and have a look at Reeves Corner. A line of cars was parked on the freeway, as lookers got out to see this sight. It was a gaunt spectacle, a blackened skeleton of a building burnt beyond repair, waiting only for its final demolition on Wednesday. Further up the road, West Croydon was still a mess, still littered from the previous night's mayhem, with shut off roads and police everywhere. Back through Thornton Heath the long line of late-night stores was shuttered and silent, and as I turned into our road, I saw that our local Tesco Express had remained closed, with shattered window panes not yet replaced.

As I finally arrived home, there was no space to park the van, as the neighbours were having a garden party. Music boomed out from across the fence, accompanied by the click of dominoes and vibrant Jamaican accents. Our cats were nowhere to be seen. I guess they don't like reggae music.

Wednesday 10th August

My daily Bible reading on Tuesday morning was from Psalm 108 which includes the words, 'give us help from trouble for the help of man is useless'. That was clear enough on Monday night.

There were the wreckers, a manic and relentless force. There were the watchers, who neither would nor could do anything about the pillage. There were the police, or perhaps there were not the police in sufficient numbers to restrain this excess of havoc, certainly at Clapham Junction. Late in the day the situation was eventually under control, or perhaps the fury of looting and mayhem had run out of steam for that night.

The BBC website has posted a discussion, '10 explanations for the riots, from moral decay to excessive consumerism'. Leaving aside for now this debate, it seems to clear to me that the shooting the previous week of Mark Duggan in Tottenham and the subsequent outrage provided the spark that ignited the riots, and the self-organised gangs of young people descending on the town centres to cause trouble, fanned and carried the fire of disorder, that subsequently drew into its path all sorts of disruptive and malevolent opportunities. Without the Tottenham incident there would have been no riots; without the gangs of youths creating the momentum, there would have been no widespread destruction.

Having said that, I don't think enough attention has been given to the broad spectrum of criminal behaviour. I learned today that a local Primary School was broken into and copper stripped from the building; whoever did it seemed to have time to drag their booty into the adjoining park to take off what they wanted, leaving the debris on the grass. That was not the work of a feverish gang of young people. I noticed an art gallery with smashed windows on Battersea Rise, and I doubt that was of real interest to youth criminals, especially as adjacent shops seemed unharmed. Monday in Battersea and south London was a day with a good chance of getting away with a crime, out of the spotlight of the main streets.

We opened the club as usual today, and as well as our regular young people, others dropped by. One young man came in, who it is said was among the marauding gang on Monday, but I did not see him then. He is about twenty, and over the years has played football with us, been to the farm with his family, and joined in with many things over the years. The first thing he said when he entered was, "where are the old photos, haven't you got any pictures of me up at the moment?" I paused and then said, "let's hope that they are the only photographs of you that will be on public display at this time."

I had a call from the Recipease restaurant at the Junction to say that despite all the troubles our group of girls should still come for their cooking workshop; and so they did, and in the slightly unreal atmosphere of working in a semi-boarded up shop front they enjoyed their lesson. Business as usual.

There is a kind of what if feeling about the place; no-one thinks there will be more trouble, but what if... Consequently, people are alert, cautious, not going out so much in the evening. The Metropolitan Police are keeping 16,000 officers on duty in London until after the weekend. I attended a meeting of Battersea youth workers, to discuss whether an event in the park, planned for this Friday, should go ahead. It was decided to postpone it for two weeks on the 'what if' basis.

There is also, I think, a north and south of the railway tracks feel to Clapham Junction. Almost as if out of the estates north of the railway came the 'barbarous hordes', and out of the housing south of the tracks came the broom army to reclaim the streets and clean up the mess. It is not as simple as that, but I discern a sort of feeling from talking with some people.

I spoke with another twenty-year-old man today, who had been present during the lootings, and his comment was that what the looters didn't stop to think about in their frenzy of theft was that when some of these High Street stores are forced to close, and the Junction declines as a business concern, it will be their mum, or aunt or brother who no longer has a job.

136

Back to Psalm 108, the context of the words quoted above is that the people are in trouble: 'who can lead us? Is it not you, O God, you who have cast us off? Give us help...'. Some of the phrases of this Psalm are identical to Psalm 60, whose words seem apposite to our situation. 'You have shaken the land and torn it open; mend its fractures, for it is quaking. You have shown your people desperate times ... Give us your aid, for the help of man is worthless.' It may have been Clapham Junction, and other places, that have been fractured, maybe something in the social fabric that has been breached, but there is a deeper ruin here. Maybe all the ten explanations on the website debate are valid – the culture of social entitlement, social exclusion, lack of fathers, spending cuts, weak policing, racism, gangsta rap and culture, consumerism, opportunism, technology and social networking. Maybe they all played a part, but all the time we fail to see that prior to any of this there is a spiritual breakdown. We avoid exploring our social relationships in the context of God, of his word, of his ways, of a deeper foundation, both personal and social.

Thursday 11th August 2011.

Things are getting back to normal today. I took a minibus load of young people swimming and ice skating, and the riots were hardly mentioned; though one girl did say that she hoped they would not start again at the weekend. I said that the momentum had passed.

Things are getting back to normal today. England seems to be comfortably winning in the cricket against India, with both the bat and the ball; but just in case, the Spurs Premier League game is postponed this weekend.

Things are getting back to normal at the Junction, at least as normal as can be expected. Traffic is flowing, trains are running, and people are on the move. Some shops are carrying on with trading despite unrepaired windows and wooden boarding, some shops are busy refitting, some shops appear to be silent, one or two shops will be silent forever.

Things are getting back to normal, but the helicopters still hover overhead from time to time, and each time you hear a police siren you ask what's up. Police minibuses still slowly patrol the area, and of course the courts are queuing with hundreds of cases, following the growing number of arrests around the country.

Things are getting back to normal. A full moon shines with an uncertain light through silver clouds this evening as I drive home through south London.

Friday 12th August 2011.

It has been announced that another man has died from the riots, an elderly man beaten up for trying to put out a fire in some bins; this in addition to the man shot in Croydon on the first night, and the three men mowed down by a car on Wednesday. There was one fatality in Battersea, though police are saying it is not connected to the recent disorder. A man was killed by falling masonry as he sat outside a bar in Battersea Rise. The building is now boarded up, with notices of condolence and a bright array of flowers. In its way it is an epitaph to the troubles, as is the message board at the Junction that many people have written on, including in other languages, including with some appropriate Bible texts.

This afternoon, I agreed that Providence House could host a forum for young people's views about the riots; local youth leaders brought along a handful of members, and it was led by the locality Youth Service manager. Maybe forty young people were there, almost half of whom had walked down the road from the mosque. Clearly they had not participated in the lootings and some of these young Muslims spoke very eloquently, expressing coherent views on justice. Equally clear was that one or two of the young people present had been there on Monday night, and may have been more than bystanders, and clear too that they had not grasped the moral enormity of what had happened. Overall the views expressed in that brief hour predictably mirrored the broad sweep of public opinion, echoed on every phone-in radio programme every day this week, and touched on the weakness of the police and the good work of the police, on the undeniable wrongness of the looting and the broader social perspective. Nothing defining was achieved that afternoon, but perhaps it gave opportunity to let some views out, and was an indicator to me that in the future we should be holding more of our own forums with young people.

The Prime Minister has spoken: 'We will not allow a culture of fear to exist on our streets. And we will do whatever it takes to restore law and order and to rebuild our communities'. The bishops are now speaking: "I hope there'll be at least some recognition of the serious and relentless erosion of public values, including those whose roots are in the rich heritage of religion. The result of their disappearing is a moral deficit in private and public life that has spawned acquisitiveness and dishonesty."

The riots were said to be copycat after the initial outburst. There are many copycat instances in broader society of what the bishops call 'spawning acquisitiveness', in expenses scandals, over inflated celebrity and sports wages, the disappearing trillions in the banking sector, and now this copycat greed without mercy at street level, almost a re-enactment of some violent play station game, only this time the points scored at each level being booty taken, crimes committed, destruction and damaged lives. In addition, the destructiveness of the looting is plain to see; less plain to see is the self-destructiveness, that the looters have looted something of themselves, something within is being lost, if not already lost.

Thirty years ago, almost to the weekend, there were riots in Battersea, two nights of them, as part of another wave of urban lawlessness. I can distinctly recall three features among rioters then, deliberate confrontation with the police, and underlying resentment against police and authority and that was the night to bring it out, and of course the chance to loot. Perhaps it is a sign how things have moved on, that it is the latter that is most prominent, accompanied by a greater crescendo of violence. A friend reported to me overhearing a couple of looters in a side road off Clapham Junction, having stopped in the street with their goods, and one saying to the other that he had left his shooter in the shop, and must go back for it.

Legislation will be hurried through in the coming weeks, as it was in the last generation, and improvements to security, policing, and maybe to social justice and cohesion; but you cannot legislate the heart. Even the call for improved education and training can only smooth things until the next time. As unfashionable as it seems, I believe it is the inner man that needs transformation. I find it very interesting in the gospel, that on one dark night a politician came to see Jesus to try and get his head around the phenomenon of Jesus' impact upon ordinary people, and Jesus said to him, 'you must be born again'. You cannot bring it about by legislation, any more than you can catch the wind. There must be an inner transformation. Over and over again Jesus did something good for someone's physical or social or domestic situation, but beyond that he did something transformative in that person's life. It is the 'beyond that' that we need today.

On Saturday night I drove from Providence House through Clapham Junction at around 10pm. The bar on the corner was throbbing to the sound of music. People had overflowed onto the street. The Junction was thronging with people, crisscrossing the road, many, many groups of people. I almost needed to take as much care driving through the gauntlet of pedestrians, as it had been the previous Monday, only this time there was no fear, only noisy enjoyment. The same was true of Battersea Rise, and then Balham, and Streatham and onto Norbury – such a contrast from the ghost town of earlier in the week. It was like all the bad dream of a few days before could be drunk away, or eaten away in a restaurant, or laughed away and forgotten. Is this what the Prime Minister called reclaiming our High Streets, or is it trying to forget that we face more than repairs and renovation, more than crime and punishment?

I drove on listening to the sound of Bruce Springsteen groaning out his song:

> The sky was falling and streaked with blood, I heard you calling then you disappeared into dust.
>
> May your strength give us strength
>
> May your faith give us faith
>
> May your love give us love
>
> May your hope give us hope

Monday 15 August.

Last week was the week of the gangs; this week the big gang is back and they want their payday. Police vans, often in threes, are seen driving purposely down a street, no doubt with a specific address that they are going to visit with a heavy hand. The council have now passed onto youth workers mug shots of looters caught on camera with the request that they be identified. It may have all stopped, but it hasn't.

I met a guy I knew from Providence old days. He was a drummer. I told him that Rock Bottom, the music shop in West Croydon, had been totally ransacked. We talked as you do, and he said from his window off Lavender Hill he saw men carrying televisions and stashing them behind the wheelie bins while they went for more. Wherever there was opportunity there was crime it appears.

I wandered up to the Junction to read the message board outside Debenhams, where about twenty feet of boarding is covered with messages, mainly affirmative about the spirit of Clapham, (and some notes to insist this is Battersea, not Clapham!), expressions deriding the looters, some Bible verses, some weird sentences, some messages to reflect on social justice. It is certainly a focal point with people stopping all the time.

I popped into see Ulrika at the Bible bookshop, to say that I was sorry she had suffered damage, and glad they were ok. She said it had been a real mercy. Someone had thrown something burning into the shop, and it singed about 6 inches of carpet, but thank God burned out quickly, or they would have been up in smoke.

Police are now sending photographs by email, circulated via the Council, of apparent looters. I reckon I possibly recognized someone, and thought it unlikely she would have been involved, but then who knows.

Back home I wanted to sit outside to read and think, but Chris was next door in his garden sort of singing like a wannabee rap star, and wafting his 'sensemenia' over the wall.

It is not always easy to think.

Chapter 11:

Day of Days

It is still 2011. September. The memory of summer riots is fading, but reasoning and questioning continue, and the soon to come recession fuelled cuts to youth service funding, almost counter intuitively.

I am in the Providence House car park. There were one or two pigeons also. It is another good place to gather. A squirrel or two, and a robin at times. And people. Of course, people. I spoke with a lady, with whom I touched elbows, as she held her shopping in both hands. She said that her son who had made some bad decisions, was now on a better path, and working in a law firm. She thanked us for our support at the time. She spoke of her other son, still hoping for that break of fortune that will make all the difference in his sporting career.

I sat against the cycle bars in the car park and made three telephone calls about a local tragedy. One with a friend of the family, one with a mentor of the family, one with the mother herself, whose son was ripped away from her so violently, so young. We spoke quietly, and about support, and about holding together.

I stood in the car park, as a tall man walked past. He stopped, we talked. We talked about his benefit application, that we had helped with, and when he should chase it up. He talked about his mother, who he hadn't talked with for over a year, but he had met with her, and it was a good contact. I noticed a bruise on his forehead and some damage to his eye brow, and looked quizzically at him. All he said was that stuff happens. Things happen in life, and he gave me that distant look.

I suppose that is it. Things happen. We can all say that. Things happen, and shrug our shoulders.

I now sit in the office, with its window onto my little world of people passing by. It is Monday morning at 9am. The office window seems dirty in the autumn sunshine. Outside is the huge figure of Stuart in his black duffle coat, hood up, leaning against our wall, talking noisily to a nervous little man called Hughie, as they wait for the Red Cross to open. It is a Monday morning routine. They are always here, always waiting, volunteers, both with needs: Hughie small and scared, Stuart big and loud. Sylvie, the manager, arrives and she is loud too,

Pam is now here, the lead teacher at the PRU in Providence. Whenever she arrives, she sings in a high, soprano voice, 'Good morning, God's Providence'. She does it every morning. She is charming and deeply concerned for her pupils. Soon she comes to borrow the phone. One of the pupils last week was arrested. Quite a few local young men were arrested last week; it is a gang related thing. This particular young person she has given so much time to, she has worried about him, prayed about him, even dreamed about him. Now she is earnestly talking with his mother trying to find out more about his situation, prying below the surface, pressing for answers. She takes these young people on her shoulders and in her heart.

Margaret walks by with her stick, slowly does it. She is going to a tenant's planning meeting in the café. Last time she went she collapsed. Hopefully she will be alright this time.

Michael comes by. He is our odd job man. I am holding some money for him. He'd like it today. I give it to him, a wad of notes, trying not to look like some back street dealer. He is going for a day out. To Balham, gateway to the south as they used to say. Then he will take a leisurely walk home; if he can still stand up.

At lunchtime, I cross over the road to Piggies, the Portuguese café, to say good morning to Joe, the proprietor, and to order some food. While I am waiting, I sit and talk with Bill, a cheery old pensioner, who despite his severe kidney problems makes sure he gets about. We talk about his life, born and bred in Battersea. On leaving school he took a bicycle round delivering for The Evening Standard. At 18 he was called up to the army and spent five years in India with the signals corps. My lunch is ready, we will talk again.

Jamel is here. He has been staying for several weeks at his aunties, to whom he is always lending money, and being helpful. He is sleeping there on the couch. Last night she pointedly told him he must start paying rent. He was affronted, took his stuff, including the television he had lent her, when one of the sons smashed their own one in a fit of anger, and returned to his one room nest in Tooting. Hardly had he told me all this and settled down to do something at Providence, when his mum called. Could she borrow £100 for her rent? Jamel too kind to be wise has gone to the cash machine to withdraw the money.

A tousled haired man sporting a high jacket presses his nose to the window. I have never seen him before. I go outside to greet him. 'What do you do in there?' I tell him about the youth programme, that at that moment a school is in the building, and am about to talk about Sundays, when he says, 'you've got it all wrong. The largest section of the population is over 50, and you're just catering for kids. You've got it all wrong, and straddles off.' Well, he's got a point.

I am glad for people who bring us down to earth, who when you think you've cracked it, push you further to think more. Elizabeth Braund always did that. Perhaps I am glad that there were no easy compliments in the culture of Providence House. It helped

145

with thinking that we have not quite got there, and there is still more to do. Something about an unfinished work. Youth and community work and faith mission isn't like a building project, roof on, and off to the next site. There is always something more, and then more again about this sort of work.

It wasn't in the way of young people to compliment you for what you were doing. Often their thanks were in the form of coming back, of wanting more. It wasn't until later, when they came back to see you as adults, that the compliments or recognition came, and then it came over and again, and came from those who mattered: those whose lives had benefitted, and then when they came to realise it, they often want to say it.

Thus it was somewhat of a surprise to receive a letter in May 2011, that read 'the Prime Minister has asked me to inform you, that having accepted the advice of the Cabinet Secretary and the Main Honours Committee, he proposes to submit your name to The Queen. He is recommending that Her Majesty may be graciously pleased to approve that you be appointed a Member of the Order of the British Empire (MBE) in the Birthday 2011 Honours List.'

I was, of course, touched. Family and close friends were touched. As I sought to process this and consider the delight and prospect of a visit to the Palace for the investiture, I saw it, and still see it, as a reflection of working in this community, and of being constantly engaged with a host of different people over many years. I saw it as being as much about the people, whose lives I had shared and served in, as about anything else. That there is something of the people's medal in this award. I did subsequently learn of some of those folk, who had collaborated to press for this recognition.

Kind words were said over the days after it was announced in the press. Ray Henry, an extraordinarily gifted youth worker, who died far too young, wrote, 'Sir Robert, in my eyes and many others in Battersea, respect is due to you every time; for all the good work you have done in our community; so you have our order of distinction: Sir Robert.'

Denise, who served as my local authority Youth Officer, said: 'Robert is a gifted and talented youth and community worker, who is able to engage at all levels of the local community to bring people together for the common good. Within the locality there will be very few people who have not come across Robert, through the work he undertakes at Providence House. He is well respected within the community by both young and old.'

A family member wrote to me, 'Wow, that's wonderful news, and very well deserved. We are sitting here with tears in our eyes sobbing, we are so pleased!' And Doug, who we used to collect in the minibus for Providence throughout his junior years, and as a man returned the favour, driving minibuses regularly to the farm, said: 'Congratulations on your MBE! you really deserve it, not only for your work at Providence and in Wandsworth, but also for putting up with the unexpected challenges all these years.'

There is an element of truth in that, because putting up with, being resilient about, is all a part of the qualification for working in the community. There is a sense that unless you can take it, you won't be able to make it, let alone shake it.

There is an irony in all this, that never ceases amuse, if not bemuse me. There was enough that summer to occupy me without thinking of my date with the Palace. There was a big project at the farm in June, when we celebrated Elizabeth Braund's ninetieth birthday, and that event was a gathering of so many different people, who represented not only her story but the twin story of Providence and Shallowford. August was full of summer programmes and social upheaval. The irony comes in that the week I appeared at the Palace for the award, was the week that

147

Wandsworth Council Youth Service announced their proposed cuts to youth provision. On the one hand I received recognition for the work we had done at Providence House, and the other hand we were told that from the next Spring our funding would be cut, and my post would cease to exist. It was always irony for me, and never a hint of bitterness.

The local authority review paper stated that 'it is time …..to shift resources away from clubs and projects that have evolved over time, but may no longer be viable'. The implication was that at this time 'the youth world that has changed and is changing', and as part of that changing environment such a place as Providence House would struggle to survive. Struggling to survive – that was always going to be the challenge for a youth charity, but survive we had, and in a note to the youth officers, I predicted we would outlive the youth service; which effectively we have.

In a letter I wrote to the Council, I said that 'we believe that the very qualities that make our work distinctive, even if numerically we have currently seen numbers decline, are the same virtues that will provide the strength for moving forward: the work of Providence House has a deep and long community heritage and high standing of goodwill; we are reinforced by the generational succession of children following parents into association with us; we have long cultured a sense of identity at Providence, where people feel they belong, that they are part of the place; we have the travelling together with East Shallowford Farm on Dartmoor which on so many levels makes a big impact on people; and underlying all of the work is faith, not just faith in what we are doing, but faith in God whose place this is, and whose lead we need to follow.'

I continued, that 'we remain unconvinced also that "the needs of young people who may feel disenfranchised will be better served by this (new) model", (quoting the Council's own review); but that on the contrary the social disturbances of August 2011 and the repeated difficulties occurring on the estates around Winstanley serve rather to underline the importance of local centres that are 'there' for young people

'For us it is essential that our youth work is set in the context of a community, of where young people come from, of where they belong. This is beyond a neighbourhood concept, as we have found that belonging is also an interior understanding. The nagging concern that we have over a one-dimensional youth strategy is whether it has the inner engine power for the long term. The heart of youth work lies in relationships and not targets, in belonging and growing and not the multiplicity of activities. We believe that the holistic context of the youth work at Providence House will open up for us a passage of growth into the future, with our open youth work, travelling in partnership with East Shallowford Farm, set in the context of a community centre, and undergirded with the principle of our Christian mission.'

There! I've said it now, and that is the nearest I have come to a theoretical framework. What's more we were still here in 2012, and still here in 2023, to celebrate 60 unbroken years of youth work in and around Battersea.

Back to the Palace. Wednesday 12th October 2011. Day of Days. This ought to the day of days, a day among days. My reading in the morning was from Psalm 121: 'I lift up my eyes to the hills – where does my help come from? My help comes from the Lord.' That seemed a good perspective.

Autumn had brought dark to both ends of the day, and London was grey after the night had gone. The slender lilac was rattling the fence in the wind, twitching its leaves in nervous anticipation. Quietly the house awoke, quietly the house prepared for this day.

The rattling continued. This time the sound of scaffolders banging their pipes in the neighbouring road. Was this the beginning of a new phase in the work, or the clanking down of a finishing project?

We drove to Providence House, the whole family, smartly dressed for the occasion. Michael Brown walked past and called out, where are you off to, looking so smart? To see the Queen? Yes, I reply. 'bout time too' he called as he carried on.

We caught the 9.16 train to Victoria.

I think: I am less worried about the last 30 years, but more about the next 10. There is a lot to think about.

What will I say to the Queen, if she asks about the work for which I have been recognised? I have thought of a few lines. That it reflects the community I have been privileged to work in. That I have never met a young person in whom there was nothing to engage with, that we should always be looking for the spark that is in every young person. That more than ever young people need to have something to work towards, something to be, especially where aspiration is low.

Then I think that maybe it is role of the church that should become more crucial in building communities.

Victoria coach station, and you can spot the MBE candidates. Buckingham Gate. I spot one young woman in pink with a splendid hat, going the same direction. Tourists throng the palace gates, taking photos as if we were important. The quadrangle. Inside the palace the horse guards as tin statues. Waiting in the ante room with other recipients and Canaletto. Canaletto's Venice hanging on the wall. The order of service is alphabetical. I am in the last batch. The waiting, the nervous chatter with perhaps equally surprised honoured people. The standing. The queue. The Queen and my insignificant words. But it's not about the words and the moment, rather it is about the years. It is all about the years. At that moment, thirty-eight and counting. It is about the community we have been a privilege to be a part of. What better place to celebrate the richness of community than in those gilded halls.

We are whisked off to the Oxo Tower as a family treat for a meal and a London view. I want to go to St Paul's. We walk there, but we cannot enter, because there is a protest of some sort.

A bus then to Trafalgar Square, where we sit on the steps, clutching the medal in my grey suit pocket, watching the public parade of everyday people, and London, hurrying home. We have done our bit of standing in luxurious halls, with Canalettos looking down at us, and silent horse guards like tin statues, my brief encounter with **Her Majesty**, the great ballroom, with the Ghurkha guards and the Queen's yeoman standing by.

Catch an 87 bus to Clapham Junction, and genuinely surprised, there is a little reception committee. It reflects something of the current day Providence House: the Sunday Bible group, the main youth workers, Jamel and the girls group planning the next activity, Phil the carpenter, Glen the plumber, even Phil Childs the referee, and my family.

A text from Rosie's phone: 'Hi dad, I got home safely around 20 mins ago. I hope you had a great day. Seriously it is so great to see u get recognition for the work you've done, which has been a massive inspiration all through my life. Nice one. Good for you! A day to remember.'

Indeed.

Chapter 12:

Values

If you stood outside Providence House in 2023, and paused to look at the dark brown brick façade, below the line of first floor windows, you would see six large photographic boards that illustrate different aspects of Providence House life and activities. At night they are lit up, hopefully. On each board there is a phrase to represent a different value of Providence: belonging in the community, developing skills and talents, having the best of times, widening horizons, connecting to God, and finding identity.

A small group of us thought long and hard over these, sat first in the café at St Thomas's Church, Streatham, then for several sessions in the media room at Providence. For the most part, Esther Clevely, then with the title of Senior Youth Worker, Nina Dei, our Children and Families' Worker, Susan and I. We sought to tease out all that Providence had meant to people, the things that had characterised what we were, and what we wanted to be; to frame the expressions that would articulate the work we did in the community and with young people, and to use it as a measure against what we were doing. Almost as a matter of routine, any planned activity at Providence House now asks that question.

Belonging in the community. Each of the photo boards tell a story.

The first board is a vibrant group of young people, standing outside the front entrance to Providence House, some still in school uniform, obviously turning up for an after-school session, and a handful of parents, with Esther in the back row, and two core youth workers in the front, Kirsty holding baby Malachi, and Trevor, aka DJ Weng Weng, hands on knees, crouched, and ready for action. Smiles everywhere, on every face. Yes, each smiling for the camera, but each beaming face messaging that we belong, this is our place, this is home, this is Providence. The caption under the picture is Belonging in the community.

The thing about Providence is that we are there. We are always there. We may not be always open, but we are always there. We were offered an option to move location, at the beginning of the consultations about the Winstanley and York Road estates redevelopment. We thought about it. We were tempted by it, but we said no. We were here. We are always here and that is a part of what people want – that Providence House is there. Still there.

Monday 30th May 2022.
It began with the bananas. We had been given a crate of bananas by a friend, left over from a local event. And some cheese and onion packed sandwiches. Who on earth eats cheese and onion sandwiches? We put out a table in the car park at Providence with a note for people to take them. Some were a bit suspicious and others eager to take. Others, most others, politely smiled and walked by.

McSweeney came past with his little daughter and I persuaded him to take a bunch of bananas. The girl was shy and clung to daddy. A Spanish speaking family came past and counted out how many of which they needed. A frail looking gentleman came and took something. I saw Vasile, who periodically sleeps rough, and he took his portion. Mostly we left people to it, and the goods disappeared. All the bananas went, but not everyone wanted cheese and onion sandwiches.

It was Bible study time at Providence, and our usual crowd of half a dozen were there. We were looking at sections from Ephesians chapters one and two. It was in some ways heavy going, because the subject matter is detailed and requires concentration. In some ways it was uplifting because it centres our life and hopes and salvation all in God, all in Christ. To the praise of His glory is the apostle's refrain, and we can't get much better focused if that is in our hearts and minds and living: to the praise of His glory.

Then Delroy banged on the front door and shouted my name. I drew him into the Bible study and the prayers that followed, which effectively curtailed the study as it was. Delroy Folkes is a burst of energy, a flood of conversation, a cocktail of ideas and thinking and memories all thrown into the air and landing somewhere, somehow. Some things he remembers clear as a bell. Other things appear to merge in and out of sequence. Some things he tells you in riddles, some things plain, or as plain as can be. He must be only a few months short of sixty, but remembers his childhood at Providence, and kept repeating the names of our founders, Rose and Miss Braund.

He has to my knowledge barely been to Providence since his youth, but this was the second time he had burst into us on a Sunday. He asked about the calendar he had left behind on the last occasion, so we gave him a new one. He gave me a phone number to call someone, so I think I will; but doesn't appear to have a number for himself. He said he had been to church somewhere so it appears he has connections in some community. We will keep in touch in some ways.

The point is we are still here. Belonging in the community.

Developing skills and talents

The second photo board is in black and white and shows the inside of the sound booth in the recording studio. The walls and ceiling are padded with a grey ribbed sound proofing. A microphone on an adjustable arm, projects from a wall. A guitar hangs from the other wall. In the centre of the picture is a head and shoulders back view of Noah, head phones on, eyes down, presumably scanning his mobile phone for the lyrics of the song he is about to record. The caption under the picture is Developing skills and talents.

Noah has been developing his skills and talents as a song writer and rapper at Providence House. He goes under the name Noaah with two 'a's, and has been part of the group of young talent that launched a music album at Providence House, has performed in various venues, not the least at a gathering for Battersea MP, Marsha de Cordova, in a room at the House of Commons. There is an anxiety combined with a seeking in his lyrics: 'what do you know about fighting battles every day in your mind.'

Noaah is somewhere along a long line of singers and musicians, who would claim some of their roots in Providence House. From a teenage Noel McKoy and the Albions, the young men of the Pasadenas, all practising their moves in the youth club in the late seventies; to the young men who probably found their inspiration in the first instance through the reggae sound systems, including local men, who still turn up to perform on request, Ziggy Anderson, Gregory Fabulous, Aston Essen. And of course So Solid, the crew of young men and women, most of whom grew up on the Kambala estate, half of whom attended the club for different purposes.

Another of that group of artists who is happy to come back and perform is Richard, known as little Richard because he was little. He lived with his family in Pennethorne House on the local housing estate, and in some of his music, performing under the name, Nu Flowah, he has sought to keep alive his grassroot links. On one occasion with a camera man to hand he climbed a ladder onto the Providence porch roof and performed his song 'Time – Life Story.'

Nu Flowah, like Noaah, won't be the last to develop their skills and talents with Providence House.

Having the best of times.

The third photograph is of three eleven-year-olds boys. They are seated in the media room at Providence House, all looking towards either someone speaking to them, or watching something on the screen. They are a wonderful mixture of reactions. In the centre is Robert, whose face has broken out into a broad grin. Robert represents modern Providence. He is from a family of boys, of which he is the oldest, and each of his three siblings have followed him into the clubs. They live in a first floor flat ten minutes' walk from the club. To his left is D'ahrya. There is a hint of a wry smile, but his focus is all concentration. He represents successive generations of Providence. His mother, Dione attended Providence. His brother, Darius did, along with a whole gang of relations on Darius's father's side. Darius Knight deserves a book all to himself, and not just these two sentences. His career as a world class table tennis star has been well documented, from inauspicious start to a more than auspicious career and development in business.

The boy to the right of Robert is Taeo, and he has half an eye towards the camera, as if to query what's going on. Ever a lad to ask a question, Taeo's much older brother was a regular attender at the clubs, when he was a boy. The caption under the picture is Having the best of times, and that is always what we want to be about.

Saturday 4th June 2022.
We had our own jubilee festival at Providence House in connection with the community and local groups that adjoin in the neighbouring passage, where the alley was buzzing with stalls and people outside Waste not Want not Battersea's zero waste hub. The event was brim full with people, just meeting, children busy in activities, community stalls, background music, live performances and, of course, food. We even had a Queen's Jubilee quiz. Faces

being painted. Children were dancing on the pavement outside the Red Cross shop, and encircled by a cheering huddle of parents.

We had a pop-up stage for performances, and interviews we conducted with people, and Gerry Ranks entertaining with his steel pans. We also had this, perhaps seeking to cover all the bases, without, we hope, fudging them, and to be something for people of all faiths and none: the pastor of the Nazarene Church spoke of building faith and community and prayed a thoughtful prayer; the pastor of the Baptist Church spoke of their new building on the estate behind, and invited people to visit; the Children and Families' Worker from the Church of England spoke – well, of families and children; the MP had a word, as did several community groups, each with their two minutes of sharing.

What it was, was this: having the best of times. We try and do that a lot.

Widening horizons

The fourth photograph is a group of children on the top of a granite rock. It is a picture from a visit to East Shallowford Farm. Half the group have hands raised and half the group appear to be shouting, as if to say, look at us! We made it, we got to the top! There is no question that these visits to the farm widen horizons. Literally as they get to see distances and vistas that London's restricted views can never give them. A Facebook post from a certain James Fox in February 2023, stated that I came to the farm 'twice for two weeks in 75 and 76 – two of the most memorable experiences of my life, a really special place.' His horizons were certainly widened. You might ask, what are we doing unless we are widening the horizons of young people, showing them the world is a bigger place than they first imagine, and the opportunities for them are broader than they had realised. The caption under the picture is of course Widening horizons.

Another extract from the diary...

"I'm not going sailing again!" "Wow! What an amazing experience!" "At least I've done it – once." "You know, I think I will remember this for ever."

August 2015. From Providence to Plymouth to meet Captain Pete and First Mate Hannah and board the SS Pegasus, sponsored by The Island (Cutter) Ltd, The Island Trust and Battersea Summer Scheme.

Eight young people, youth worker Frank and me.

Frank, with his epic strength, always making up with extra effort when the rest were flagging. Frank at the helm, then quietly crawling to one side to vomit overboard, then quietly returning to take up the helm – always ready with a joke, and his game 'a bunch of fives'.

Only Chike and Troy had been before. On the night trip back, I sat with Troy on our night watch at 4am, he huddled in his waterproofs, and I asked what he was thinking. 'I'm frightened and sitting here is pointless.' Sometimes the young people found it hard. But Troy was the first to say he would come again.

For Nathan, Marlee and Lewis the feeling sick, the challenge of different tasks, the discipline of the night watches do not appear to have been outweighed by the joys. They were each at their happiest on shore in Guernsey. We all since joked about the experience with them, so bit by bit positives will unfold.

For everyone there was something hard to take, especially the sea sickness, but for Kyle, Ibrahim and Will they seemed to rise above it all. Kyle hardly said a word, Ibrahim had very few words of English and Will never stopped talking. Kyle took to steering like a fish to water. Will had the capacity to articulate special moments: when he came off the first watch on Wednesday night, he told me how amazing the stars were; when he came off the third watch he couldn't stop talking about the dolphins who skipped by the starboard side while he was steering in the moonlight.

Ibrahim had few words, but a broad grin and the eagerness to learn and ask questions; some of Hannah the first mate's repeated cries were, 'where is your life jacket?', 'do up the crotch strap', 'strap yourself to the line'. After we restarted the youth club in September, I spoke with Ibrahim's foster mother. She then said that Ibrahim wanted to speak with me. Clearly with a twinkle in his eye, he said, 'Robert, I can't find my lifejacket!' The memories of the sea were still strong.

After it was all over, and we had returned to London, I stood outside Providence House, with a constant stream of cars flowing past. People scurrying hither and thither, and the continual hum of urban sounds. Above it all the high blocks of the Falcons Estate, like great masts in this ship of concrete. That's where we have taken these young people from, and what a contrast! Standing on the deck, holding onto the rigging as the ship swayed from side to side on the swell of the sea, and nothing as far as eye can see, but water and sky, and not a sound but the wind and the lapping of the water, and the creak of the ship. There could not be a greater contrast for these young urban kids, and although they may not yet articulate it, it forms part of an experience they will not forget, and may well lead them onto further challenges to come.

Horizons were widened. Literally.

Connecting to God

The fifth photo board that is hung above the front porch and entrance to Providence House, shows a group of young people in the front reception room seated in a circle, presumably discussing something. The front focus of the picture is the back head of a girl, with her hair plaited, and probably leaning forward. The

159

photograph is deliberately anonymous, and it would be hard to identify any individual in it. The caption under the picture is Connecting to God. That is the bottom line with Providence. We would want all to make that connection, to finding in looking for a way, they might find that Christ is the Way.

This extract is from my diary of Tuesday 9th September 2003. 'Collette popped into to say that she is to be baptised on 28th September in Southfields. That was encouraging. As a child and younger teenager, she had been very committed to attending Sunday School. One of our helpers reckoned that she had 'given her life to Christ' on a coach trip during a summer holiday club outing; but we were more cautious about that claim. She was a regular visitor to the farm growing up, and appeared in the BBC short film about East Shallowford. As she grew older, her life seemed to modulate with the ups and downs of her troubled family, and we lost touch with her; but it appears the faith influence wasn't totally lost, and she came into contact with a Christian group in Southfields. Earlier in the summer, she had bounced in to Providence to describe her personal conversion to faith. Now she has returned to announce her baptism. It is a serious, public act, so our prayer was that God grant her a lasting faith.'

Connecting to God.

Finding identity

The final picture, in effect to the right of the entrance, is two rows of head shots, with three people featured in each row. They are all young talents who Providence House has nurtured in a creative direction, and facilitated the growth of their own voices. The caption under the picture is Finding identity. Indeed, the words of some of their songs give expression to their own anxieties, their own discoveries, their own searching, and their own journeys.

There are many places where we begin to discover our identity, and many staging posts along the way. We are glad to have been one of those staging posts, and at times influence posts, along the way.

One of those in the photo montage is a young man, who goes under the name of Malachi Army, and in his song Keep True, he declares: 'I'm just trying to be true to the people, I'm just trying to keep true to myself. I hate living in a world that's unequal, confused and abused by material wealth.'

Finding identity, finding a voice.

Another in the picture is Phil, performing under the name of Deandre, and his words reflect a similar journey: 'Everyone's been asking why, why you're crying. I've been looking around searching for something. I've been trying to get help, looking for one thing.' With a chorus that goes: 'I'm not worthy of your grace, I'm not worthy to kneel before your face.'

Finding identity, finding a voice.

Chapter 13:

Untold Stories

In 2022 Providence House won a grant to fund an Untold Stories project for 2023, during which year it is hoped to capture many personal stories over the past decades and to frame them in the music that was popular at the time, and in addition facilitate the current crop of budding singers and musicians to perform. It has all the signs of being enriching, informative and entertaining.

Telling and hearing and discovering people's stories has always had a place in Providence House. Elizabeth Braund was a story teller. I have tried to be a storyteller. Around every corner is another story. In an hitherto ad hoc way we have gathered stories over the years. Perhaps this project will galvanise it into a more methodical process. At Elizabeth's 90th birthday celebration at East Shallowford Farm in 2011, we set up a camera in the porch of the old farmhouse, and encouraged people to sit in the white metal garden chair, that had been where Elizabeth's mother Lady Braund would sit on a sunny afternoon in her latter days. From that chair, people with a London-Providence connection or a Devon and Dartmoor connection gave their reflections. In 2014 at Providence's 50th anniversary, we set up camera and microphone on the Chapel stage area and invited people to tell their tale, individually or as a small group of peers. In 2021, at the Looking Backwards, Looking Forwards event we had a roving microphone and roving camera to capture more untold or half told stories.

This book, One Year is not Enough, is my attempt of telling a story, of Providence, of myself, of people with whose lives we have intertwined, and please God, too, a story of grace.

There are more stories to be told, as the life of Providence House treads its path through the differing opportunities that will arise, and the varying challenges that will present themselves. Part of that story will be Esther's story. Esther Clevely came to us in May 2012, and started her appointment as Senior Youth Worker. It must have been a daunting challenge, and a step of faith, finding her role among a quite established team of youth workers, recruited by me, and with me very much around; although hopefully stepping back meaningfully from the youth work leadership. Esther had to embed herself in the culture and values of Providence and East Shallowford, and begin to find her own voice, grasp her own vision, cultivate her own leadership style. She would be the first to admit it was not without struggles, with both steep and less steep learning curves. Ten years on and Providence House appointed Esther as Director, with a mandate to develop the creative arts as the key driver for the youth work at the centre. A short way into this programme the music culture has developed to professional standard, new explorations with art and dance and drama have progressed, and with her twin mantra of creativity and faith, Esther is set to lead the work into the years ahead, and open the way for more untold stories to be told.

If this was being written in another year a different set of names would appear on this page, but for 2023, Tracy Lenga is the Youth and Creative Arts Worker, Belinda Drysdale with Susan the children's workers, Steph Wells, Maria Newey, and Barry Ballard in operational roles, Kirsty Burgess, Ren Johnson, Trevor Isaacs, Kyron Simpson, Elias DeSouza are on the payroll as youth workers, three of whom have grown up within the youth club, and all of whom have a story to tell. Behind them is a lengthy list of volunteers.

If this was being written in another year a different set of names would appear on this page for the East Shallowford team. Julia McDade, with an extensive career in the developing world, is the Trust Manager, building on the good work of Debbie Sandels, who led the project in the immediate years post Elizabeth Braund. Will Dracup, tall, big smiling, born and bred Dartmoor, is third generation family farmer from the neighbouring farm, and leads the farm based activities for young people. David Onah, with an even bigger smile, who came for six months which was turned into a permanent appointment. Ellie Baker who has pioneered the conservation work at the farm. Arthur here for a year's experience, and we all know where a year's work experience can lead! And Serena Walcot who has covered every position in the team from Elizabeth's time until the present.

The point of this is that the story is unfinished. That is how it should be. The story is bigger than the personnel, who move on; but the story is the personnel: the story is the people.

And of tomorrow? Battersea continues to change. Providence House may well reappear in the sights of local authority area development. The building has been fit for purpose for over 50 years, and adapted internally to change as needed; but what about the next number of years. How will national challenges to faith values impact on the thinking of Providence House? How will partnerships with other organisations develop for better or worse? How difficult will it be to make choices between what is easy and what is right? Will the values that Providence House holds, forged out of years of interaction with people, continue to inform and illuminate and enhance the decades ahead?

All that story is yet to be told. I have two thoughts to bequeath. One is a cautionary note, that has been sounded in Providence House for many years, beginning with Elizabeth Braund; the other is an aspirational hope, almost *carpe diem* kind of thinking.

The very first report to Trustees that Elizabeth submitted after settling into the new Providence building in the early seventies was entitled, 'Unless the Lord builds.' She was quoting from Psalm 127, which opens with the words: 'Unless the Lord builds the house, its builders labour in vain; unless the Lord watches over the city, its watchmen stand guard in vain.' It is a kind of yardstick, a hang on, let's think about what we're doing here. What are we doing? What are our principles? Are we staying true to foundation principles? Where, quite frankly, is God in all this? Irrespective of who we work for, who we work with, this is a thread that needs to be woven into the fabric of the present and the future.

Around the time of Elizabeth Braund's death in 2013 and in the following year with the celebration of 50 years in Providence, I began quite naturally to reflect a fair bit. A scripture I kept returning to seemed to me like a window into a future. The ensuing 10 years may not exactly have grasped hold of it, but I offer it as a continued window of hope. The apostle Paul writes in the New Testament to the Corinthians. He is actually talking about that innate blindness of people to perceive what God is doing. His specific reference is backwards to Christ on the cross, but it seems to have a forward sense to it as well: 'No eye has seen, nor ear heard, no mind has conceived, what God has prepared for those who love him.' (1 Corinthians 2.9). Based on a God-given foundation there is a future to be grasped, a doorway to be gone through, new sights for the eye to see, new sounds for the ear to hear, new ideas for the mind to conceive; and this - new stories to be told.

Untold stories. To close this chapter, I submit a number of untold stories. I do this because the stories of people are core of the work, the daily cameos, the short encounters, that thread together with the administration and planning, to make it all make sense, or to have that ring of truth.

A diary extract from 2006.

They are definitely 'not the best', but they do try hard even when the odds are against them, and they keep up a fighting spirit. They were the under 16s football team. This year they will not have won any cups and will have finished mid-table. We had been trying to re-build the team, but one of the difficulties was guaranteeing a full squad to turn out. Even from the youth work perspective they are an interesting bunch of lads.

Richard cannot attend evening training, as he has a tag on his leg, his felony being in possession of a fire arm at 15 years old. Now Eugene, one of the more promising players, has joined the curfew brigade for being present, and therefore complicit, at a robbery. He was the last person to imagine slipping down that path, but we are hopeful he won't slip further. Micah also ran foul of the law in connection with bikes and disorderliness; but interestingly he has developed the most of all the team, in personality, performance, eagerness and sense of responsibility. One of the boys appears too friendly with the local gang, while another is hesitant to come training because of a gang.

Then there is 'Wrecker', who seems born to end up in an argument. In trying to actually stop a fight somewhere he was bottled over his head for his troubles. Kieron got into a fist fight at school, which the adversary tried to escalate with a knife. Kemar on the other hand is quiet, keen and dependable, and produces delightful cameos on the pitch. Steffan and Travis are equally pleasant, and regularly attend church, but are not so reliably regular to football. Each week someone or other appears to be missing. Onyema has been known to us the longest, but Morlai seems unable to get up on Saturday mornings, whatever he does Friday nights ill prepares him for the next day. The keeper is a great character, and one of life's triers, but this team needs something more than trying. Neil is promising, when he comes, having had a try out for Swindon Town.

They are not the best, but for the most part have since done something useful with their lives. **Things, too, can turn out for the better.**

At this point in the story five years have passed, and I ended up in court. Not on my own behalf I hasten to add, but for Kwaw, aka Wrecker's behalf. Kwaw, now 21, and huge, tall and erect, his jumper stretching with muscles, finely tuned during a teenage spell at Her Majesty's Pleasure. Hopefully he has gained maturity, and experience while away. Almost the day he was free, he visited Providence House with a friend one Sunday and after the usual pleasantries and embraces, came his offer, if you need any help....As it happened, we did need some help. One of our football managers was almost desperate for more support with his 16 year olds, and with rumours of incidents 'on road', as they say, was worried lest anything ever blew up during a game. Who was there to help? Try Kwaw, he wants to help, and he's a big lad.

Kwaw was pleased to be asked. He attended the first couple of games, enthused with the excitement of the football, and supported the mid-week training session. One week, the team went to Camden for a cup match, a straightforward 11-0 victory, then the tube homewards, and a storm of little incidents; a lad with no ticket, a lad with a wrong ticket, accusations of handing travel passes down the line, and Kwaw, thinking he was being helpful, adding his voice to the shouting of the ticket guard; a policeman called and in the tempest of noise and bustle he was arrested on a public order offence. I was not there, but happily driving home from the farm, listening of all things to a Beatles' CD, when Richie, the football manager's call came through.

Kwaw's trouble was on our watch, his arrest breached his licence, thoughts of him returning to prison having tried to be a useful volunteer disturbed me. So, on the Monday morning, the rain descending like a flood, I made my way to Horseferry Road, to the Magistrates court; but no, the venue had been changed, so bus and tube to the city to another court, me following behind Kwaw's mum and Kwaw's girlfriend. All morning spent listening to half cases of defendants being fined, or cases deferred, or procedures not followed, before Kwaw's solicitor managed to reach the court. Her sensible words, the magistrate's perception that this was not quite as it was portrayed, useful reference to our presence in the court and Kwaw received a fine.

Mum's text later in the day: 'Hola! Big heartfelt thanks 4 all ur prayers re Kwaw. May you be always bless! Shalom!'

Fast forward a few more years, and Kwaw is a grime artist. I am sent a music video of him performing, with another singer, set against a background of Lavender Hill and Clapham Junction, with Arding and Hobbs store behind. It is around time of the Black Lives Matter protest in 2020, and Kwaw/Wrecker is performing what I might call a protest song. It's about black oppression, suppression, survival and revival. 'Lost my brother to the street, lost my brother to police, lost my brother to the system.' 'There's a war going on outside. You can look deep in the eyes and see the distrust. Just a verbal picture you could cut and paint with a brush.' It all fits the current mood.

For Kwaw it was hopefully a case of things can turn out for the better.

Things, too, sadly can turn out for the worst.

Fivepence came to see me one Thursday morning in 2017. It was still quite early. People were still hurrying past to work. He had seen the doors of Providence open, and had called in. He said what he always said each time he visited: have I got a drink? He meant a fizzy drink, but I gave him water. He is about my height, maybe a bit shorter. But his eyes were glazed, his black skin pallid with poor condition. He had the distant look of someone on medication, or drugs. Or possibly in his case both. I talked with him a bit, trying to tease out where he may be getting support. He mentioned a recovery programme locally, and gave me a name. I gave him a card to give to one of the staff to contact me. Who knows.

Somewhere along the line he couldn't 'guard his heart'. Somewhere along the line he couldn't 'keep his eyes straight ahead'. Somewhere along the line ….

Fivepence used to play in a football team with us, but that was before he had drifted too much.

Later, that same morning, I was in the car park dealing with some lumber for the dump, when my name was called. This man was from the same football team as Fivepence. He had rolled with the same crew in his mischief days. I believed he had served some time inside, but things were different now. I stood next to him and looked up. I am five feet six (on a good day). He must be six feet six, and more, but with his construction worker's helmet on he looked even taller. We talked about Fivepence. We talked about his own work. We talked about different paths.

He bounced off down the road, and I went to the dump. I haven't seen the construction worker since, but I hope he has continued to do well; but Fivepence continued to be a regular visitor until he had to be moved out of the block of flats he lived in.

These two young men aren't the only ones to tell a story about different paths. **Sometimes, though, things turn out for the better.**

With the lift man you are almost guaranteed a smile. Possibly he learned to communicate by smiling, before he would venture into longer conversations by talking. He is almost 30 at the time of writing, and we have known him since the smallest of boys. We have a picture of him crossing a stream on Dartmoor, less than five years old, ginger haired and possibly smiling even then. There were things he didn't really do. He didn't really do youth clubs – too many children. He didn't really do school – too many children again, and probably too many teachers, or teachers always in a hurry, and probably the wrong kind of learning. He didn't do much in the way of conversation, and reading and writing didn't really grab his attention. He didn't do motivation.

What he did begin to do, slowly at first, and later on in waves, he went to the farm with Providence. He had already been there with his mother on family weekends. Then he started to go with youth groups, even though on the surface it wasn't easy to see whether he actually liked it. Something clicked, beneath the grin was a determination. Perhaps it was easier because he didn't need to write or talk about it, after all the animals were interested in neither. He grew up tall and big boned, and learned to use his weight to his advantage, discovering he could lift things more easily than others.

It would be difficult to say when he started his first paid job, but now on building sites he is a valued worker, not the least for his reliability and honesty. Perhaps the first course he completed was a sort of preparation for the workplace, three-month, hands-on activity course, in Battersea, called SPEAR, well supported by mentors and tutors. Perhaps the most regular work experience was

Providence House workparties to the farm, and annual two to three week visits to assist with lambing, with Debbie and Al acting as surrogate parents whenever he came to stay. He is now so familiar with the routine that farmer Will gives him the title 'management', at which of course he smiles. He is now first on the list for any workparty, arranging his job schedule to fit. He has invested also in his tools.

He does now do motivation. He is in fact an inspiration to men and women far older than himself. His name is Antony and together with his father, they are the go to men to support the set up and organisation of half the local festivals that take place in Battersea.

Oh, and by the way among other tasks on a busy construction site, he is a lift operator.

Here is another thought, with some stories to illustrate them. That there are different ways in which our community impacts with us and we with our community.

There are those who make a mark in the community. Susan and I we spent an evening in 2022 with the Mob Father. We even had a photograph taken with him under his banner. He reminded me that we had probably first met in the mid-seventies, so it had been a long association. We were not the only ones who spent the evening with the Mob Father, who was celebrating 60 years of a very varied life. There were dozens of people, a large hall-filling crowd. I hasten to add the Mob Father is an affectionate nickname of Freddie, someone held in wide respect by a wide range of people. By youth and community workers, by people in music, by people in sport and radio, by extended family. By many people. As the song declared – One Love.

Freddie Morrison, probably the most well-known youth worker for many years in the borough of Wandsworth, and a man who could have gone to higher things, but realised there was no higher call than to work among young people. It is good when people can come together to celebrate their connections with each other, with their shared stories. It is a good thing to be present when a man, as in this case, or a woman, feels they are comfortable enough among friends, who will affirm them, not doubt them, to state some things boldly, to share some things vulnerably, to show some things with good heart and good purpose.

As to the evening itself, there was good food, good conversation, a pair of steel pans playing, two singers who performed songs of hope, a promotion of a worthy charity, and several short speeches from the Mob Father himself. I was privileged to be asked to pray at the outset of formal proceedings, and the work of Providence House was mentioned in despatches during the course of the evening. It was good to renew acquaintances with a number of people, but most especially with one with whom we have stood together in this local community over many years.

That was a large gathering, but most of the sentiments above can relate to small groups that we all link to, or operate within. We are all connected somewhere. His is a well-loved story, but it can equally important when people, less well known can celebrate their own steps forward.

There are those for whom the mark they make is small but just as important

It was just before Christmas 2017, and he was pleased as punch on this day. I had known him for forty years. A rough and ready man. Tells it how he sees it, even if you don't want hear it how it is said. He likes a drink, and then he likes an opinion even more, and then even less you might want to hear it. He was a worker, mainly on the tracks for the underground, and earned his pension. He regularly came to Providence with his unmistakable Jamaican accent, mixed up with his London voice, his free comments and generally asking for me, Mr Robert.

On this day he was pleased as punch. Dressed smartly with a navy overcoat, striped tie to match his striped shirt, shiny polished black shoes. And an envelope of papers. Proudly, or was it still beaming with relief, he took out his British citizenship certificate. The night before at the Town Hall, along with other eager adults, he received his certificate from the Deputy Mayor.

He came to Britain like so many others as a teenager, and built his life here, schooled, worked and bred; but all the while using his Jamaican passport to travel with. Now things are different. The last two times he asked me to write a reference, that he took with him in case customs questioned his right to return. Now he has sought for the paperwork to prove what in all intents and purposes has been his identity for most of his life. He is a Londoner, that has been his home, and now he has the papers to prove it. On this day he was as pleased as punch, and now he wanted his passport application countersigned.

He was not a popular man, or a well-known man, like Freddie, but he was known to his family, known to his circle of friends, and he knew who he was: a Londoner, a British citizen. That is the story of Carlos, and it is important to him.

There is always the belief that change is possible.

It was a Friday night. It was probably in the summer, but it was a long time ago.

It was the usual large gathering of young people and young adults at Providence House, for the regular reggae music event.

It was one of those evenings when you knew something might kick off. There had been trouble in the area the weekend before, and the word was that some people would come to wreak revenge and that it might take place at Providence. Then we got a tip off that this group were on their way.

I walked around the back of Providence where I knew some of the local guys were gathering, and went up to a couple of them, and said that we had heard this group was on its way, and I didn't want trouble in the club. I asked what was their policy? With a tensed, set, po faced look one of them replied, 'there is no policy'. He unzipped his leather jacket and took out a shot gun.

I turned prayerfully back to the club, probably more in hope than faith. As it happened when the posse of angry men arrived, there was little more than some bravado, a swish of a sword to intimidate, a menacing dog on a short leash. The group brashly walking into the entrance of Providence and threatened dire consequences. Outside a flourish of weapons and the visiting group, on realising they had bitten off more than they had planned for, slinked back to where they came from.

Many years later, I attended the funeral of the man with the leather jacket. A large number of the Battersea Caribbean community were out to pay their respects. I had known him on and off through the intervening years, his years of wildness, his years of working, and a bit of his years when work mixed with other issues that marred his life. I believe he had lived alone for the last few years or so, before his terrible accident. After three months in hospital, he finally passed away.

At his funeral he was surrounded by his large family, including one son in handcuffs, another on day release from prison. One of his daughters spoke clearly about her father's latter days, about how on the day of the accident there was an open Bible on his bed, and about how in the hospital in his last weeks she believes that not only did he come to faith, but had begun to ask what his mission in life might belatedly be. His recurrent phrase apparently was 'finish the race.'

It may never be too late to start the race, but it is always essential to finish it.

On the day I wrote this chapter, it was international women's day. A local community worker friend had been interviewed on local radio, and was asked who were the inspirational women in her life. My friend, via WhatsApp, asked me who would be the inspirational women in her life. Without hesitation I would say it is Susan. In May 2023, it will have been forty years since we first made our promises to each other. It will have been more than forty years since Susan first volunteered at Providence, and she has done it all with imagination, fortitude and grace in almost every position. That is as a true volunteer. Without hesitation I can say I thank you for the companionship and the being togetherness. Thank you for the patience of love, the persistence in grace, and the devotion in faith. For motherhood. For good decisions. For promise keeping. For partnership in mission and family. For that knowingness and understanding. For that sure touch and sound thinking, and thank you for the knowledge of wild flowers to enrich every journey we have taken together. I haven't even started to tell her story.

If you were to visit Providence House any time after 2014, you would be able, if you walked slowly enough up the main staircase, to see a series of story photo boards about the work of Providence House. As you climb the steps, so the story turns with you. As you reach the top of the steps, there is one more display. It is a mirror, and you look in it. It is there as a reminder that you are part of the story, and perhaps your story needs to be told.

Chapter 14.

No need to put the fire out

Without a doubt Battersea has seen many changes over the last 60 years. I write this in Providence House's sixtieth year as a youth charity. Sixty years ago, you would have stood in this neighbourhood and seen a very different picture. The Winstanley Estate itself was just beginning to be built, but there were none of the wide sprawling housing blocks, such as many of our members have lived in on the York Road Estate. The whole locality was a grid of old Victorian terraces, scarred by dilapidation and pock marked by bomb sites from the war, and where children still scrambled among the rubble. There was no Providence House Youth Club as we know it today, but rather the amazing Miss Braund had already begun the vibrant work with young people in the old Providence Chapel on the corner of Speke Road. Neither the chapel nor the road are there any more. In fact, where some of current Providence families live is just a stone's throw from the old Providence. On the site where the current Providence House now stands on Falcon Road was an old public house. The final years of the sixties witnessed further re-development of the neighbourhood as high rise and low rise blocks rapidly rose out of the rubble. The old Providence Chapel was almost the last building to be demolished, and we have photographs of the Chapel surrounded by demolition on every side.

When I first arrived at Providence in 1973, the new purpose built Youth Club had been opened for just over three years, on the main road, but dwarfed by the tall blocks of the Livingstone Estate. By this time the York Road and Livingstone Estates seemed to seamlessly merge with Winstanley as one swathe of concrete running from Falcon Road to Plough Road. Kambala Estate, the other side of Ingrave Street, had still to be developed, along with the modernisations around Maysoule Road. There were no riverside developments then, and I can remember walking from Battersea Bridge to Wandsworth Bridge calling in at all the factories from Morgan's Crucible to Price's Candles in search of a part-time job to supplement my volunteer expenses at Providence. When the west wind blew you took in the Battersea smell from the fumes of Garton's Glucose factory and the brewery. Bit by bit so many things have changed. Where the chemist is on Falcon Road, we used to walk into David Thomas department store. Where the flats at 134 Falcon Road are now, used to be the Queen Victoria pub. Around where Haven Lodge sheltered homes are located, I used to be sent to Thacker and Paul's, the hardware store, for screws or nails or whatever. So many changes, but so many people have longer and richer memories than I have. This generation will now experience the great upheaval for themselves, and walk past places where this used to be and that story took place, and tell it on to the future. In every regeneration there is gain, but there is also loss. It will be interesting to read the verdict in years to come.

I lived for my first ten years in Battersea on the job – in Providence House; but overall, I have worked for over fifty years in this neighbourhood and still counting on. Maybe the biggest changes have been the people. When I first arrived, the old traditional community was being broken up, some families remained in the area and were housed in the new flats. Many families moved away, and in their place came a much more ethnically diverse population. The grandparents of many of our present youth members would have been in this new wave of inhabitants coming into the area. During my first years I witnessed at first hand the difficulties people and young people had in adjusting in a short space of time to new people and places and to people from different backgrounds. Sometimes it was tense, sometimes it was tentative, but, hopefully also, Providence was a place where different young people could meet and get on and find a sense of belonging and roots. The perception in those early days was of a growing community of white British and Afro-Caribbean families finding their way forwards; but since then, the diversity has, of course, bloomed, and with each phase of habitation the diversity grows. To add to the cultural diversity also came the economic one, and where in the past the young professional would have sped past Clapham Junction in the train to the suburbs, now they compete for prices in the housing market in Battersea. Every morning you can witness the daily hurry past the window at Providence House, the great mixed congregation of people rushing to the station, the bus stop, the school. On the surface a glorious mixture, but I suspect not far beneath we see many lives lived in parallel rather than together.

For many years my office was a window on this passing world. I would sit there, at my desk, computer on, with the window half open, and engage by watching, or engage by talking with the many who stop and chat, before passing on again.

In May 2014, Providence House celebrated fifty years of working in this community of Battersea. On that day from 11 in the morning until 11 at night there never ceased to be a trail, and at times a flood, of people coming into look, or participate, or catch up with people they hadn't seen for years. It was like a snapshot of Battersea over half a century, with people from every intervening decade of the life of Providence and of this community. It still moves me to think about it today. Some weeks before the event we spoke with a man, who turned round and said, 'Providence House has been a part of our lives.' That became our strapline for the celebration and has been so ever since, that in small ways, in big ways, in fleeting ways, and in life changing ways, Providence has been a part of so many lives.

They say that young people don't use youth clubs today. It is a thing of the past. They have said it before and will doubtless say it again. It's a bit like saying young people don't need each other, or young people don't need challenges, or shared experiences or the opportunity for new things or simply the space to be and to be together.

I have met so many families and been able to be a part of so many lives. Attending weddings and funerals, and over the last few years conducting many funerals for Providence people, and helping families navigate a pathway through grief and hope. Attending christenings and being a godparent, to the sons of two men, whose lives deeply entwined with ours at Providence. I have to admit of not being a devoted enough godparent to these two, now adult men with their own lives to lead. Part of that was that I seemed to be a kind of godfather to so many young people. Supporting the transition from youth to work, writing references to help towards acquiring the next post, or in some cases to help avoid a prison sentence. Being there for advice, or to share stories and experiences. Part of lives interacting together.

Part of the richness of the experience for me has been knowing several generations of a family.

There is Christian Gordon, for example, for whom I wrote some of the above words in the foreword to a council sponsored photo story he undertook about the changes in the local area. A very thoughtful short book that captured both the hope and anxiety about change. With Christian, and some others, I was also involved in the making of a film, carried out using pupils of Falconbrook Primary School, Wye Street, Battersea, as part of a reflective record of redevelopment and change. This excellent documentary has been showed from time to time on UK television, entitled 'Battersea Junction', an oral history of Winstanley and York Road Estates, and produced by Matthew Rosenberg, an affable and gifted documentary film maker.

Christian lived only a few yards from the old Providence in Holcroft House, a long tower block, where many Providence families lived. He would have kicked a football, had he known, above the very earth on which the chapel had been built. His mother, Brenda was in the first cohort of a girls' group that Susan and I ran. His father, Steven Gordon, Flash, was from a local family. His mother's siblings, all nine of them attended Providence at some point or other. Tony was a gifted guitarist, David was a football star, Barry's son is a key member of Providence youth club, Clive has a career in some kind of youth work, and Marlon the lorry driver has driven for us on numerous occasions. The older siblings represented Providence House in earlier times. Grandmother Mavis came to our wedding, and to Elizabeth Braund's surprise eightieth birthday in the village of Widecombe in the Moor. Mavis was a part of the generation that came from Jamaica to begin a new life in Britain, and made it her home and the home for the family she established in south London.

Christian himself helped pioneer the beginning of our music recording and creative performance work at Providence House. Memories of a young Christian, his curly hair, bright smile, gliding in on his segway board, relaxed, intelligent, with ideas above his youthful age, with hope and aspiration, representing the youth of today and tomorrow; but also, the citizen, maybe one day a spokesman, who knows.

In 2012, I retired from leading the youth work at Providence House, and ceased paid employment as the local authority funding for my post ceased from April that year. I didn't retire from Providence House, just stopped being paid. Thankfully the teacher's pension I had signed up to in December 1976, and had done with hardly thinking about it, now came into action; but I wasn't about to leave something that had been such a part of my life, and that together had been such a part of so many lives. I didn't retire from Providence House, just changed my role. I styled myself

Director of Youth and Community Work, which seemed a sufficiently catch all title. I found myself having more of a trustee role, as after the death of Elizabeth Braund in 2013, we began to think through more clearly trustee arrangements, the muddle of Providence House being two different trusts; one the original faith trust, the other a sort of subsidiary youth trust. I slipped into having more of an operations and building role, the one part I think I am glad to finally have let go of. I found myself, again post the passing of Elizabeth, far more involved in the workings of the farm as a charity, becoming the chair of the Shallowford Trust.

I had one or two other local projects I had already got involved with, being a governor at Falconbrook School, to which I think my most valued contribution was taking school assemblies, and a trustee of the Trinity Fields Sports Association, to which my most valued contribution was organising an annual primary schools football tournament on their lovely green fields, which I ran for seventeen years. Both of these I gave up as I felt I could no longer give proper time to them. The one thing that being theoretically retired I did find time for was a local funded project called the Big Local, which in the immediate area close to Providence House began in 2011 and will finish in 2025, and will have spent a £1million plus on local community projects, including the vibrant Falcon Road Festival which ran for several years. I have fulfilled a function in this group as chair, treasurer and advisor of sorts at different times. What it most did for me was to discover more community networks and connections in the neighbourhood, and hopefully be a part in tying some together to be stronger, to be as we coined a phrase, Battersea Together.

I was also, until his death in 2012, heavily involved as a trustee and supporter of my father's charity, The Musgrave Collection, a most curious museum of art and exhibits that mirrored the image of his eclectic life and interests. In a number of ways, I regret its passing, but then perhaps it had its brief day. His extensive collections of St Paul paintings, all his own work, are stowed in bubble wrap in my brother John's attic space.

It is the thing with charities and organisations fired by one person's imagination that they often come to notice with a flourish. One such organisation I have been lured into, in part as a partner with Providence House, is Waste not Want not Battersea, led by the impassioned Hadas Hagos, and for which I have served as a trustee. Combatting food waste, feeding the hungry, inspiring community, it has been a nourishing and nurturing local organisation to be involved with.

In December 2021, I did, however, more formally retire. I had already handed over director to Esther, but from that point on I ceased to be on the staff team. Except. That is the problem, or perhaps the joy. Except for being a trustee. Except for being involved on Sundays. Except for being part of the East Shallowford structure. Except for being around to advise. Except for special projects, such as in the Providence sixtieth year. There will be a time when the exceptions will diminish. Except for this: Providence House – a part of our lives.

In December 2021, we held an event at Providence House, entitled Looking Backwards, Looking Forwards. It was a celebration of the work we had all done together. It was a looking back to those days and years many of us had shared together, but also a looking forward, with today's and tomorrow's leadership and direction. There was still the threat of Covid-19 lingering, but we felt it sufficiently okay to stage, and in part glad that it kept potential numbers from getting out of hand.

The car park at Providence sizzled with a huge paella cooking, and music to draw attention to what was going on. The six new photo boards beamed down on the groups of people coming and going, and taking pictures of each other and of old friends, and to get a picture with Robsky. Pimm trailed around with a long microphone seeking to capture folk who had a story to tell. Inside the building around every corner someone seemed to be serving food. Along every wall, on every table and on every movable screen appeared photographs, to tell the story of the past fifty or more years, and as ever someone would say 'where is the picture of me?' The media room showed a continuous loop of Providence films, and visitors came who represented different stages of this journey we have travelled, some who had come from a distance, some who had walked from around the corner, some like the team from East Shallowford who had travelled up in convoy. In the first floor sports hall with stage open we held two performances in which people representing several decades of Providence demonstrated their talent. Children danced and the twins, Savannah and Sienna read their poem about peace. Ziggy, Gregory, Nu Flowah, Aston, Deandre and Esther all sang.

Helen, brought up in Battersea, who had visited the farm as a schoolgirl in the 1970s, volunteered at Providence in the 1980s, and moved to a new life in Devon, close to the farm in the 2002, looked after the memory book, which as in 2014 began to fill with rich memories and comments.

Nu Flowah wrote, 'Thank you for playing a big part in my life. Going to Providence was like winning the lottery in the early eighties! You are a legend.' Shaquiel wrote, 'Without you a lot of friendships wouldn't have formed. You brought the whole community together.' Charmaine added, 'Where to start? Thank you for so many years of education, activities, holiday trips and so much more. Most importantly for introducing me to my faith at the age of 4. Thank you for all the love you have shared among the community, and for rescuing us all on a Sunday afternoon, 2 o'clock sharp for Sunday School.' Dennis wrote, 'You are a true inspiration to generations and continue to inspire. We will never forget what you have done for the community and me personally.' Lynch, to keep a bit of perspective said, 'I remember playing for Providence football team, and being left at Waterloo station as I missed the train home. Great memories!' I often see Lynch walking towards Clapham Junction station, so hopefully his time keeping has improved.

Seon Ifield, who was a steward on that day, remembered that he 'was just passing by, when Robert appeared, and invited me to come in – and the rest is history.' Daren, aka Sardo, and has worked in partnership with Providence, wrote that 'I've known you since I was 10, and you've always had time for the Mandem.' Brenda, Christian's mum said that 'no words can express what you mean to the Graham family, and thank you for all the wonderful memories over the years.' Paul Graham, no relation, wrote about life change: 'So here is to a great man who has inspired many to change lives, their thinking…I was stubborn, but Robert asked me do you not want to change Paul, and he showed me love, patience and tolerance.' Some kind words, that despite repetition illustrate the importance of sharing the journey. In fact, our Providence House mission statement talks about walking with young people and families in their life journeys.

My brother, Peter, messaged me the day before the event. He is a hidden songsmith, who produces melodies for family occasions. He wrote a song that said 'it's time to go, it's time to retire; we don't need you now to put out the fires; get out while you can, and people admire, the work that you've done and what you've inspired.' I haven't gone yet. I am still about, but in the words of Malcolm Hunter, best man at our wedding, and great friend and colleague over many years, 'make room gracefully.' I hope that I have been doing that. Making room, allowing the leadership of others to grow and blossom.

I have tasks still to do. Still play some part in this community. Contribute more to celebrating the story of Providence House and this local story, and that of East Shallowford and its enriching connections. I have a secret walk-in cupboard in Providence House, in which is housed every record, every photograph, every report that wasn't digitalised, and if I manage the time, then out of that hidey hole will come more stories and more reflections of this thing that has been … a part of our lives.

I will re-surface, however – a bit like the river Falcon. I've always been fascinated by the river Falcon, long, long ago lost to ground level. In centuries past, it carved a little valley with shallow hills on either side, as it ran down what we have long since called Northcote Road and Falcon Road. I remember when I worked in Woolworths in the 70s that the basement lift used to flood each autumn, and we were told it was the river rising. I was told too that Providence House is built on a concrete raft, and the blocks of the Livingstone Estate on great columns deep into the soil to allow for the movement of water in the Falcons little flood plain. I was told that somewhere, now underground, that the Falcon swung left-handed along what is now Ingrave Street, underneath where York Gardens is, but will sometime be swept away in this next wave of regeneration, to the pumping house from where the Falcon brook finds its way into the Thames, beyond Battersea Reach.

But every day the Falcon River resurfaces, but most people are unaware of it. The buildings opposite Providence House along Falcon Road from time to time have trouble with the underground stream and its movements. The undertakers, however, have a pump in their basement. Every day like clockwork it starts, and to manage the levels of water below, they pump out pure stream water from the side of their building. It is a wonderful sight to see the fresh water slipping out onto the pavement and draining away, even for a short while.

I, too, will resurface from time to time, fresh as the Falcon brook.

A few last words before I stop putting out the fires.

185

The first date was the tenth of December 1951 at Smith Memorial Hospital, Brickdam, Georgetown, Guyana. The name of the hospital, and I am not sure if it is still there or whether it has been renamed, is shared with Smith Memorial Church, also in Brickdam, and which I believe still holds that memorable name, and where my father was minister in 1951. The church was erected to the memory of Reverend John Smith, a London Missionary Society Minister, who was sentenced to die by the British colonial authorities for the role he allegedly played in the historic East Coast Demerara slave insurrection of 1823. John Smith was a white man working among black people, so maybe the connection has a stronger significance than just the name.

It was on a Sunday evening in September 1965, that a teenager made his peace with God. Although having been brought up in the faith, and been bred into the example of faith and following, it was then that he was awakened to the need to find faith for himself and not slip into the shadows created by the faith of others. It was a decision hopefully more than that made by a boy, but that of which the apostle John writes: 'born not of natural descent, nor of human decision, but born of God – and to all who received him (the Christ), the Father gave the right to become the children of God.'

It was on a Tuesday evening in July 1973, that a young man began hesitantly at a Christian mission working among young people in south London. A hesitancy that turned into a constancy and into a vocation. A youthfulness that grew into manhood, and familyhood and fatherhood, and leadership and hopefully a way of working characterised by coming alongside, and in that way sought to mirror the coming-alongsidedness of the Saviour, who would be there as the example to always follow.

Many seasons have passed since then, and amidst 'all the changing scenes of life, of trouble and of joy', please God, 'the praises of my God shall still the heart and tongue employ.' (Nahum Tate). Now the season of turning has arrived, that time of full circle, that time where it can be said there has been 'every activity under heaven' (Ecclesiastes 3.1).

That point too where it can be repeatedly said, 'so let's make our steps clear that the other may see, and I'll wait for you. If I should fall behind, wait for me.' (Bruce Springsteen).

This, too, holds true, has held true, and in faith remains true, as the prophet of old said: 'Whether it is the bread of adversity or even the water of affliction the Lord gives you, you will need the teachers no more, as with your own eyes you will see it. Whether you turn to the right or to the left, your ears will hear a voice behind you, saying, "This is the way, walk in it."' Isaiah 30.20-21.

The best thing then is to keep walking.

Robsky's Rap: Part of our lives

Been here 50 years, had some hard times, shed a few tears.
I came for one year, but it ended as a lifetime.
Providence House a part of our lives, part of our lifetime.

In 76, Miss Braund picked up sticks and started a farm,
East Shallowford Farm, A Lung for the City,
Heart of the Matter, pitter patter.
Providence House part of our lives, part of our lifetime.

Seventies, eighties, nineties, working in community,
Kids clubs, football, music on a Friday,
Bible on a Sunday, Youth on a Weekday, clubs in the holiday,
Best time of our lives.
Providence House part of our lives, part of our lifetime.

In 81 the locals rioted, got nicked by the police who said I'd started it.
One night in the cell probably did me well -
At least it gave me street cred.
Providence House part of our lives, part of our lifetime.

In 83 I started a family,
Two girls and a boy who brought us joy.
Battersea Balham Norbury -
It's all the same for me,
Same line always on time.
Providence House part of our lives, part of our lifetime.

So Solid crew, twenty-one seconds to go,
SUK that's for another day,
A new generation more tribulation,
But still the same jive,
Providence House part of our lives, part of our lifetime

In 2011 got the MBE, Her Majesty the Queen pinned the badge on me;
She shook my hand and said Robsky wha goan?
I told her how it is and she said 'so long'.
Providence House part of our lives, part of our lifetime.

Providence values like a light, Providence values keeps us right:
Connecting to God, connect to community;
Widening horizons, Finding identity;
Developing skills and having the best of times.
Having the best of... having the best of ....having the best of times
Providence House part of our lives, part of our lifetimes.

It was 2021, and my time was done.
Time to make room for younger ones;
Looking backwards, looking forwards;
Providence House part of our lives, part of our lifetime.
Providence House part of my life, part of your life, part of our lifetime
Looking **backwards** looking forwards
Looking **forwards** looking backwards

Looking backwards looking forwards
Always looking keep on looking backwards forwards…..

A part of our lives.

One Year is not enough

by Robert Musgrave

To read more about the work of Providence House, you might like to read:

'The Young Woman Who Lived in a Shoe' by Elizabeth Braund MBE.

If you have enjoyed reading this book, you might also enjoy other short books by Robert Musgrave, available on Amazon:

'To be a Pilgrim' – 10 days, 21 companions, 18 reflections in the Holy Land

'Words in a Lockdown Year' – A perspective on a lockdown year.

And available at Providence House:

'Looking Backwards, Going Forwards' – Thinking aloud with Psalms 150-139.

'Chasing after the Wind – 100 Days with Ecclesiastes.

All available from Providence House, 138 Falcon Road, London SW11 2LW.
info@providence-house.org
www.providence-house.org

All profits from these books go to The Providence House Trust. Charity number: 1181473.

Printed in Great Britain
by Amazon

26895765R00109